A Tutor's Guide

Helping Writers One to One

Edited by
Ben Rafoth

Boynton/Cook Publishers
HEINEMANN
Portsmouth, NH

Boynton/Cook Publishers, Inc.
A subsidiary of Reed Elsevier Inc.
361 Hanover Street
Portsmouth, NH 03801–3912
www.boyntoncook.com

Offices and agents throughout the world

© 2000 by Boynton/Cook Publishers

CIP is on file at the Library of Congress.
ISBN: 0-86709-495-8

Editor: Lisa Luedeke
Production service: Lisa Garboski/bookworks
Cover design: Jenny Jensen Greenleaf
Manufacturing: Louise Richardson

Printed in the United States of America on acid-free paper
05   04   03   02   01   00   DA   1   2   3   4   5

Contents

Making a plan helps to keep the writer's priorities in focus—but how do you know when to stick with the plan and when to scrap it?

Being helpful can become too much of a good thing when tutors cross the line and take over the session. There are signs to watch for and ways to pull back.

No tutor can be completely prepared for the ways that emotions play out during some sessions, but you can learn to deal with them by acknowledging feelings and then forging ahead.

When a writer won't talk, it's hard to make anything work. Experienced tutors understand this reluctance and how to address it.

Tutors can tell a story to thaw the ice when a session seems to be going nowhere, and it doesn't have to be long or profound.

What's so hard about proofreading? Spotting errors isn't as simple as it seams.

Technology has made plagiarism easy, but tutors can steer students away from it by showing curiosity and enthusiasm for the writer's ideas.

Here are some familiar and not-so-familiar resources for tutors, including works about language, the culture of conversation, and the personal sides of writing.

Topics for Discussion
Ready to do something about bad assignments? Does your campus ensure due process for students accused of plagiarism? Here are six topics related to the chapters in this book that ask you to consider your role as a tutor in the greater college community.

Acknowledgments

I would like to thank many people for their support and encouragement along the way, but most especially the contributors to this book who made it all possible. Thanks also to Mickey Harris for helpful feedback on the proposal, to Beth Rapp Young and George Cooper, Kara Bui, and Linda Riker for early completion of their chapters for the proposal, to the National Conference on Peer Tutoring in Writing, especially the 1998 conferees at SUNY Plattsburgh, some of whom are represented in this collection, to Katie Bailey and Doug Tucker for help with typing and proofreading, to Jen Ritter for Web site design and typing, to Lisa Luedeke, my editor at Heinemann Boynton/Cook whose encouragement and guidance have been invaluable, and to my family for love and kindness always, Mary Ann, Henry, and Paige.

Introduction

A Tutor's Guide offers a way to take everyday events in tutoring sessions and connect them to theory and good practice, not in a comprehensive or encyclopedic way, but in a manner tutors can relate to. In these pages, you will find conflicting ideas and glimpses of the scholarly debate—the stuff that enlivens teaching and makes it a thinking person's job. But mainly, you will learn to deal with the problems that arise in tutoring sessions by using effective strategies and exercising good judgment. The goal of this book, then, is not to provide answers but to help you think through problems and gather new perspectives on them. It does so by opening the door to some of the professional conversation that surrounds writing center practices. At the same time, *A Tutor's Guide* offers concrete suggestions and things to do and think about for the next tutoring session. This is basically the same approach to problems that writing center directors and other composition specialists seek, and it seems fitting that tutors participate in this community of teacher-scholars as well.

Each chapter in this collection is organized in a similar manner:

- *Introduction*—Describes a specific problem or concern that you are likely to encounter in writing conferences, like trying to engage a reluctant writer, helping to make a paper more creative, or dealing with an emotionally charged session.
- *Some Background*—Explains the problem further and puts it in a context of theory and practice, including clear explanations of current ideas from the professional literature.
- *What to Do*—Offers concrete suggestions for how to approach the problem and what to try when that doesn't work.
- *Complicating Matters*—Raises counterarguments, exploring some of the complexities of learning to write and why "effective tutoring strategies" don't always work.
- *Further Reading*—Recommends helpful and interesting follow-up readings; includes a short description of each selection and its relevance for tutoring.
- *Works Cited*—A complete list of references for each chapter.

At the end of this book you will also find *Topics for Discussion*. Topics cover several different areas and each one poses some thought-provoking questions and possibilities for discussion in staff meetings, for entries in a tutor's journal, or just to ponder. They invite you to imagine what your center might become as well as what the center means to the students you serve.

Every one of the authors writing for *A Tutor's Guide* is now or has recently worked in a writing center. They are the voices of experience. Contributors to this volume include recent undergraduates who have presented their ideas at national conferences on peer tutoring, graduate students who are now in law school or working on their PhDs, faculty directors of writing centers and writing programs, authors, and editors. They are the voices of writers and teachers.

And who are you? The authors of this book had to imagine, but they have given it a good deal of thought. Probably an undergraduate or graduate student working part-time in a writing or tutorial center for the past several months or more, a pre-service teacher, a curious and thoughtful person who likes to talk about ideas and enjoys helping others, and an excellent-but-ever-growing student and writer. Even if you're not all of these things, you know the role. And that's who the authors of this book tried to imagine: readers who can envision themselves becoming ever more engaged, more curious, more thoughtful about what happens when they meet with another person to help him or her with writing.

Each chapter in *A Tutor's Guide* focuses on a problem or concern that you are likely to encounter in your tutorial sessions. In fact, this book focuses on the most common problems tutors said they face—and some of the hardest to deal with. While your Top Ten list of difficulties may differ, this book will surely cover some of your concerns. We all know tutoring is about much more than solving problems and that no two sessions are ever the same, but it is the common problems, often encountered on a daily basis, that get our attention and raise our curiosity levels. They create a motivating dissatisfaction, a need to figure out what is happening and how to deal with the problem the next time around. This, in turn, makes us wonder about what our problems have in common, how they may change or shift when seen from different angles.

The authors of these chapters try to meet you near the front line, pull you back about fifty feet, and help you see how a problem as you experienced it might be framed as part of a larger conversation about tutoring, teaching, learning, and writing. They believe—based on their years of experience—that this conversation is the path to discovering new knowledge about writing and about yourself; and this is what makes working in writing centers an integral part of your education. What you will not find in this book is any presumption that there's a magic wand that will make problems disappear, or that any tutor would be so gullible as to think there might be. The authors of *A Tutor's Guide* are close to where you are now but also a little farther ahead, and they invite you to hike with them, use your head, take some risks, and realize that all tutors are part of a much larger world of writing theory, research, and practice.

A final note. Ideally, every writing center should have its own Tutor's Guide written by and for its own tutors. This book may give you and your colleagues ideas for things to write about. I'd like to hear about your own center's Tutor's Guide and the discussions you have related to this *Tutor's Guide,* so please let me know. And if you have comments for the authors included in this volume, send them to me at (brafoth@grove.iup.edu) and I'll forward them along. Comments on the book may be viewed at <http://www.chss.iup.edu/wc/guide>.

1

Setting the Agenda for the Next 30 Minutes

William J. Macauley, Jr.

When you meet a writer and sit down to talk about a paper, it might seem a little odd to make a plan for how you will spend the next 30 minutes together. But there's a worse problem: looking back at the past half hour and realizing you went practically nowhere with your tutoring session because you never really thought about where you wanted to end up. Every tutoring session needs a plan that the writer and tutor can focus on, even if you wind up changing it along the way or scrapping it completely.

I like to think of this plan as similar to charting a course on a road map. A road map is open ended in that it shows you many possible routes to travel, but the specific course you choose on the map never lets you forget that you're on a purposeful journey to your destination. Charting the course for a tutorial session is also a way to mark, simply and graphically, the things you want to do in the tutoring session: "Begin the session with _____, then _____, and conclude by _____." Fill in the blanks as you wish.

Years ago, I delivered a truckload of greeting card racks to a department store in Johnstown, Pennsylvania. I had been making my living then as a driver and it felt exciting to be going over-the-road. Shortly after crossing into Michigan, I pulled into Ma's Coffee Pot in the late afternoon before my trip and pored over the shiny new atlas I purchased there, computing the mileage and deciphering the lines, circles, dots, and colors that marked my route from Michigan to Pennsylvania. I marked my route, got a good night's rest, and started out early the next morning.

Well, anyone who has ever driven on an expressway in western Pennsylvania (especially in a truck) knows that having a map is no guarantee against wrong turns and traffic jams. Low bridges and narrow roadways are a problem,

SEE DISCUSSION TOPIC #5 AT THE END OF THIS BOOK

too; I learned that firsthand when I ended up backing the truck around blind corners and up hills, blowing my horn into the darkness, and turning around to find another road to Johnstown. But the route I marked with a yellow highlighter always kept me focused on where I had been and where I was headed.

More than once I tossed my atlas on the floor in frustration (truckers hate to ask for directions), but I finally backed up to the store's loading dock just before ten o'clock the next morning, road weary and sore. Two languishing humpers (freight handlers) met me in the parking lot, unloaded the racks from the truck, and I was off to the nearest Motel 6.

The point of this story is that planning a trip may not be the last place where a journey is negotiated; it does, however, give travelers a sense of perspective on where they are and where they want to end up. It is easy to lose this perspective during a tutoring session because the ideas in a conversation go by so quickly. My marked-up atlas kept me oriented and moving in the right direction even though it could not predict all the specific problems I encountered as I traveled; the map was necessary but not sufficient. It kept me aware of my options yet focused on my goal.

For a tutorial, charting a course for the session means setting the agenda for how we want the session to unfold. You and the writer might begin with a plan as simple as this:

> Brainstorm (10 min) → Pick out main idea → Write thesis statement

Or your plan might be more elaborate, depicting problems the writer asked for help with early on, and others you decided to add after reading the rough draft. You could just make a list of these things, but mapping them out on a separate sheet with arrows (as I did above) keeps the plan flexible (you can add to it easily) and gives it an appealing visual dimension. It is also a drawing that you and the student can make together.

Some Background

What I'm mainly talking about in this chapter is making a plan for the tutoring session, but you can also make one for the paper itself (like an outline). Many current writing textbooks include substantial sections on planning an essay through tools such as:

- "building blocks"[1]
- clustering[2]
- mapping[3]
- outlining[4] or
- the "reporter's formula"[5]

Mapping, whether you do it for the whole paper or for the tutoring session, is a particular form of planning that lays out your main points and connects them with lines or arrows. It doesn't have to be hierarchical like an outline; instead, it can take the shape of a hub with spokes, a continuous circle, a tree, a flowchart, or anything you want. It not only fixes a sequence of ideas or events in your mind but also provides a visual representation that can be used to help you stay on track—or take a jaunt. A tutorial map lets you point to the specific events you want to happen during the next 30 minutes, and you can add or delete a path, as well as insert placeholders, question marks, or reminders. You and your writer (Joe, in the example below) might make a plan for the session that looks something like this:

Think of illustration?

Decide how Joe's main idea compares with article's→Figure out main diff→Rewrite intro

Check quote

Like flowcharts and bar graphs, maps are visual representations using terms that do not have to be a part of the student's paper. So it's ok to jot down something like "Emphasize main diff" on a map until the writer figures out the exact words he wants to use in the paper. One of the advantages of drawing this kind of map in a tutorial is that it can be negotiated. When the map is negotiated, it is multivalent, meaning that both the tutor and writer can plan the tutorial cooperatively without either dominating the session or being tied unproductively to the writer's text. You can even think of the map as a third participant in the way it mediates the practice of the tutorial, affording an egalitarian or common space for working together and reminding us, as Paulo Freire says, that "Communion in turn elicits cooperation."[6]

Another way that tutorial maps function is to change the language options in the session. Tutors sometimes find themselves sounding like talking heads about writing because they don't really have a plan for approaching the writer's work and end up doling out generic advice ("Remember your audience," "Transitions are really key"). Student writers, by comparison, sometimes find it hard to apply what tutors say because the comments are not concrete enough. The opposite can happen, too: tutors can become editors because they don't know where else to begin, while students lose sight of their ideas because they get caught up in minutiae. When the agenda is set collaboratively with a map, however, the phases of the tutoring session are made explicit so that there's a better chance for mutual input and understanding. I hate to compare tutoring to going to a dentist, but I will anyway to make the point that I always want to know what my dentist plans to do before he does it, and I appreciate it when he loses the fancy medical jargon and just draws me a picture or shows me a diagram. I think the same holds true in the writing center: students want to know what's happening and they want to be part of any decision.

One more point. Tutors are often more skilled at conversing than the clients they serve. For one thing, in the writing center we're on our home turf and they're not. As a visual representation, a map does not require conversational skill. If the writer has trouble speaking up or changing the topic, she can point to the map to signal her intent. Or she can revise the map while you're talking or reading her paper. The map is always there to go back to.

Experienced tutors are adept at dealing with papers from many disciplines, courses, and teachers. But when tutors and writers map out a session, the plan can soon outlive its utility. So while setting an agenda is useful for conceptualizing a journey based on available information, you can never know what the trip will be like until the rubber meets the road. How do you decide when to stick to the map and when to take a chance on an alternate route?

What to Do

Setting the agenda for the next 30 minutes (or 45–50 if your writing center has longer sessions) will most likely be a variation on this general framework: Review the assignment, decide on the goals for the session, and finally, choose the best route to reach these goals.

Beginning

Before trying to build an agenda, ask open-ended questions about the paper and assignment. If you intend to encourage a student writer to take responsibility for writing, do so from the start of the session by asking him to tell you what he is thinking, what he wants. Is this the writer's first visit to the center? If so, begin by telling him about your writing center and how tutoring works. Then try to decide on the primary goal for the tutoring session. Is it to clarify some aspect of the assignment? To identify problems with the writer's supporting statements? To develop a stronger sounding voice? Exactly what is it that you hope to accomplish in 30 minutes? Write it on the top of a blank sheet of paper.

Setting the Agenda

Explore options for how to proceed. This is where your expertise as a writing tutor is really important. But I recommend that you begin by inviting the writer to tell you how he would like to proceed. If this doesn't take you very far, suggest some options. Keep the primary goal in mind and look for the most direct route to reach it. (Other chapters in this book offer lots of ways to address specific problems and concerns that writers bring to the center.)

Draw the map together. Offer the writer a pen or marker, something with a cool color and an irresistible rollerball feel, but don't insist on it if the writer doesn't want to try it. Drawing a tutorial map is not everyone's idea of fun. Encourage the writer to help you name the points and connect them, yet realize that you may have to compress what she says into a map format.

Warn the writer of time constraints. This one is a little sneaky. Make sure that you tell the student that the two of you might not get to all of the points identified. Let the writer know that he may have to carry on alone, after the tutorial session has ended. This is when you tell him how useful the map will be later on. The sneaky part is that the agenda is almost more important for the writer's work after the tutorial has ended because the ultimate goal is always to enable the writer to work successfully without your help. You will have modeled how to make a plan, and this will go a long way in empowering the writer.

Complicating Matters[7]

In my truck, I was not constrained by how much vacation time I could afford. Rather, my travel was shaped by how long my employer expected the trip would take. This metaphor plays out in important ways for writers and tutors, too. Students are seldom working on only one project at a time, and the writer must have the opportunity to discuss time constraints. If the paper is due in 20 minutes, he doesn't really have time to explore the region; he just needs to know which exit to take.

I would encourage flexibility here and also warn that the faster you drive, the more likely a crash. The urgency of the writing is often a result of not getting started early enough, and the tutorial session can often be a student's attempt to let a tutor make up for lost time. That lack of foresight is not the tutor's fault or problem; meanwhile, you still want to help. So, as a tutor, you have to decide where the cutoff is for you, at what point covering some ground is less important than facing the consequences of delay.

The student may view the tutorial as nothing more than a quick fix on the way to turning in the paper within the next hour. Is it more useful just to get him on his way or do you really want to tell him the importance of pretrip tire pressure inspections? If you try to push students beyond their time constraints, you run the risk of assuming too much responsibility for the student's work and turning the writer off to tutoring. This is an example of what Wingate (this volume) calls "crossing the line." We would like everyone to be working through drafts with enough time to be thorough and thoughtful. Meanwhile, we know that this is often not the case. At times, we can almost see writers flashing their brights behind us, trying to get us to move out of their way. If we help them to move along, we may be able to get them into the garage again before their next trip.

Some student writers are just not interested in exploring their topics, regardless of the amount of time they have. They are focused on getting the paper done with sufficient success, like earning a B−. Gregory Clark suggests that this is the difference between a tourist and a traveler.

> Tourists engage only the places and people they can recognize as belonging
> within the boundaries of the territory they themselves occupy, but travelers
> leave that territory behind as they transform themselves in response to the ne-
> cessities of the experience they encounter on the road.[8]

A writer may desire nothing more than returning to what is safe and familiar, like writing about how playing football builds character or how school uniforms deny individuality, and it may not always be productive to push a writer beyond his own planned route. You have to ask yourself, will pushing make him challenge himself and increase the likelihood of good writing? In other words, what is the upshot of forcing a student into an adventure through the mountains when what he wants is a straight shot to the coast?

In *Zen and the Art of Motorcycle Maintenance*, Robert Pirsig talks about the Zen of motorcycling—knowing your vehicle, hearing and feeling the operating condition of the engine, and knowing the viscosity of the oil as the engine runs. Most writing tutors and teachers yearn for students to pay this kind of attention to writing, even though it would probably put them out of work. While it would be nice if everyone thought about writing with this sort of intensity, as a tutor you may feel that only you, not the writer, thinks about writing this way. In fact, you may be so attuned to what the writer needs to do that you skip the important step of spelling out the agenda and negotiating it with the writer. In other words, you may think, If I know the problem is in the crankcase, why discuss it?

But it's a mistake, really, to presume that you understand better than the writer what the session needs to be about. The map is not the tutorial. It is, rather, a plan for what the tutorial might be, a way of paying attention to one thing so that you can focus on another. And so what seems obvious to you may not be the case at all once you begin to see things from the writer's perspective. This is why negotiating the agenda and making the plan explicit is so important: it gives both of you a turn at the wheel.

Moreover, getting through the agenda may be less important than setting it because it is here where tough choices must be made. In 30 minutes, there may be only enough time to get to the first couple of points, but the writer leaves with a clear sense of what to do next. Ellen Barton observes, ". . . reading and writing often play less of a role than the talk that comprises the encounter."[9] Planning the session thus becomes the means to helping the student work with her writing both now and later on, so that what happens in the writing center actually reaches into the student's future.

In order to meet the needs of both tutor and writer, that communion which Freire points to must be remembered. I would encourage three approaches. First, keep revising the map so that new considerations can emerge and be accommodated. Though mapping a tutorial is a very smart way to begin, the work of a tutorial is often not predictable enough to allow that map to remain essential throughout the session. Second, if the map becomes cumbersome, drop it.

As I said before, the map is only as good as it is useful. Sometimes, it is better to explore than to plan. Finally, there may be times when the map is more useful than the writing the student has done. Let the writer take that map, make it her own, and hit the road.

Further Reading

Flynn, Thomas, and Mary King. 1993. *Dynamics of the Writing Conference: Social and Cognitive Interaction*. Urbana, IL: National Council of Teachers of English.

This collection of essays accomplishes several goals important to agenda setting in tutorial sessions. First, it focuses on describing and promoting higher-order concerns. Then it looks at collaborative writing from different perspectives. Tutors will appreciate the discussion of writing and writers in practical terms.

Murray, Donald M. 1995. *The Craft of Revision*, Second Edition. New York: Harcourt Brace.

This is a good book to read when you need ideas for planning the agenda with writers who seek help on problems in focusing, organizing, developing, reshaping, finding a voice, and editing. In a clear and entertaining style, this well-known author and writing teacher gives useful advice and concrete examples that will help you make suggestions and explore options to plan constructive tutoring sessions.

Rico, Gabriele Lusser. 1983. "Chapter 11: Less Is More." In *Writing the Natural Way: Using Right-Brain Techniques to Release Your Expressive Powers*. Boston: Houghton Mifflin, 236–59.

This chapter is useful for tutors who want to use visual representations, like clustering, and it offers new ways of talking about topic, purpose, and audience, which writers will appreciate. This chapter is also quite helpful in the way it weaves together writing-to-learn, the entire process of writing, and the idea that there are multiple participants in each text.

Notes

1. Christine A. Hult and Thomas N. Huckin, *The New Century Handbook*. (Boston: Allyn and Bacon, 1999).

2. Ann Raimes, *Keys for Writers: A Brief Handbook*. (New York: Houghton Mifflin, 1999).

3. Leonard J. Rosen and Laurence Behrens, *The Allyn and Bacon Handbook*. 3rd ed. (Boston: Allyn and Bacon, 1997).

4. Gary Columbo, Bonnie Lisle, and Sandra Mano, *Frame Work: Culture, Storytelling, and College Writing*. (Boston: Bedford Books, 1997), 29.

5. Max Morenberg et al., *The Writer's Options: Lessons in Style and Arrangement*. 6th ed. (New York: Longman, 1999).

6. Paulo Freire, *Pedagogy of the Oppressed*. 20th Anniversary ed. (New York: Continuum, 1994), 152.

7. I would like to acknowledge Janice Sebestyen's comments on an earlier draft as the basis for this section of the chapter.

8. Gregory Clark, "Writing as Travel, or Rhetoric on the Road." *College Composition and Communication*. 49 (1) (1998): 16.

9. Ellen Barton, "Literacy in (Inter)Action." *College English*. 59 (4) (1997): 409.

Works Cited

Barton, E. 1997. "Literacy in (Inter)Action." *College English* 59 (4): 408–37.

Clark, G. 1998. "Writing as Travel, or Rhetoric on the Road." *College Composition and Communication* 49 (1): 9–23.

Colombo, G., B. Lisle, and S. Mano. 1997. *Frame Work: Culture, Storytelling, and College Writing*. Boston: Bedford Books.

Freire, P. 1994. *Pedagogy of the Oppressed*. 20th Anniversary ed. New York: Continuum.

Hult, C., and T. Huckin. 1999. *The New Century Handbook*. Boston: Allyn and Bacon.

Morenberg, M., et al. 1999. *The Writer's Options: Lessons in Style and Arrangement*. 6th ed. New York: Longman.

Pirsig, R. 1974. *Zen and the Art of Motorcycle Maintenance*. 10th ed. New York: William Morrow.

Raimes, A. 1999. *Keys for Writers: A Brief Handbook*. New York: Houghton Mifflin.

Rosen, L., and L. Behrens. 1997. *The Allyn and Bacon Handbook*. 3rd ed. Boston: Allyn and Bacon.

2

What Line? I Didn't See Any Line

Molly Wingate

It can happen in the middle of a tutoring session—maybe at the end. The pleasant exhilaration of working well with a writer is replaced by a queasy, uneasy sense that this session is not going so well after all. You may notice that the writer is relying on you, waiting for you to do or say something. Or you may notice that the writer has disengaged from the tutoring process, waiting for you to stop doing and saying. Either way, the session is no longer productive, and the weight of it is on your shoulders. When did the shift occur? When did this session slip over the line between being writer-centered, process-oriented, and effective to being tutor-centered, product-oriented, and fairly useless? How could you, an experienced tutor, have missed the crossing? Where is that line? How do you find it? What to do when you have crossed it? These are the guiding questions of this chapter.

Some Background

Most tutor training texts begin their conversations about tutors and their roles with the assumption that the job of a writing center is to "produce better writers, not better writing."[1] Of course, we do not have to sacrifice better writers for better writing or vice versa. Toni-Lee Capossela points out, "It's possible to make better *writers* AND [emphasis in original] better writing, but not if the writing is made better by another hand."[2] For a tutoring session to be considered productive, it is essential that the writer does the bulk of the work and learns something that can be used in future writing projects. As tutors, we know what our goals are, but sometimes it is hard to see the line between only

SEE DISCUSSION TOPICS #4 AND #5 AT THE END OF THIS BOOK

demonstrating to the writer what could be done with a paper and teaching the writer to do those things on his or her own.

Figuring out how much help to give "can be personally troubling," as Christina Murphy and Steve Sherwood note. "The natural tendency to be helpful and supportive may conflict with a sense that doing too much of the student's work will not produce the desired result. . . ." [3] Here are their suggestions for how to proceed in a session:

- Give a candid opinion of the strengths and weaknesses of the work in progress; in the process, be sensitive to the student's reactions.

- Suggest ways to enhance the strengths and minimize the weaknesses in the student's writing.

- Recognize that every text and every writer is a work in progress. [4]

These suggestions can help a tutor negotiate the territory between helping and hindering.

In addition to guidelines for proceeding in a session, many tutor trainers discuss the roles that tutors can play, or as Leigh Ryan puts it, the hats that tutors wear—the ally, the coach, the commentator, the collaborator, the writing "expert," and the counselor. [5] Each of these roles is rich with possibility, just as each is fraught with potential line crossings. The tutor's task is to combine the suggestions for proceeding in a session with the roles tutors can play to create and maintain a tutorial that stays on safe ground and helps the writer. I have been tutoring writers in writing centers since 1981, and I still struggle mightily to create and maintain this balance.

What to Do

In staff meetings at the Writing Center at Colorado College, we talk about sessions where the struggle didn't turn out so well. In the beginning, tutors learn to spot when they have or are just about to cross the line in the most obvious situations. If a writer asks a tutor to proofread or edit the paper, we explain why we would rather teach proofreading. When writers try to pump us for information about the paper's topic, we can tell them in all honesty that we do not have the information they seek. And although plagiarism has many nuances, we have lots of tricks to subvert the writers who would love to copy down our every word. We can give them a variety of choices, give examples that are parallel but not appropriate for the paper, or give suggestions faster than anyone could possibly write. Once we have tutored for a while, these obvious situations are predictable, and we have quick, graceful, and face-saving ways to respond. We know that every writer and every situation calls for a different approach, and we know how to improvise within a set of guidelines.

Brainstorming Sessions

The line becomes obscure when the tutorial session is focused on the ideas of a writing project. A tutor can begin to wonder whose ideas make up the paper that comes out of a session. This more subtle form of line crossing comes up often in staff meetings but has few pat responses. Take the situation of helping a student who has trouble extending ideas. Perhaps the tutor shows a writer a brainstorming heuristic that generates a lot of material. The tutor then joins in the fun of debating both sides of an issue and helps the writer answer the who, what, when, where, and how of a topic. The writer comes out of the session with a great deal more material, and it seems genuinely insightful. Coming up with critical material for the paper was the purpose of the session, but the tutor wonders whose work it was. Did the tutor collaborate or commandeer? The same question can arise when a tutor suggests a tool for analyzing a draft that results in a radical reorganization, vastly improving the paper. While the tutor and the writer are no doubt happy that the paper is improved, who did the re-organizing and did the writer learn anything about being a better writer?

When a session is focused on the ideas of a paper, tutors can lose track of their role and step over the line. Many tutors talk about how they suddenly realized that they were doing all the work in a session, that the writer hadn't talked as much as they had, or that the writer did not look or sound confident. They realized that they were no longer teaching the writer something to use in the future because they had become too involved in dazzling the writer with the possibilities they saw in the paper. The writer, along with the tutor's role as teacher, had been left behind as the tutor pushed onward toward a better paper, not a better writer. These sessions were no longer effective.

The "Over" Sessions

There is yet another category of tutors crossing the line that creates unproductive sessions. I call them the "over" sessions: overempathizing, overwhelming, and overtaking. In staff meetings when we talk about problem sessions, tutors find the over sessions the most troubling because they aren't sure when they crossed the line into unproductive territory or whether they could have avoided it. The tutor sees that a writer is quite distressed with a professor, for example, so the tutor decides to listen, even sharing experiences with similar teachers. The writer goes on to give a history of every experience of writer's block since third grade. The tutor feels sure that the writer needs to talk about these blocks to get started. The writing project is forgotten, the session is almost over, the paper is barely begun.

By *over-empathizing,* tutors can make it hard for a session to be productive. In the example above, the tutor assumes that the writer needs to talk before he or she can start writing—probably a safe assumption. But when sharing experiences did not move the session along to the current project, the tutor should have changed directions. Talking about past writer's blocks did not help the writer overcome them, while writing something might have. The tutor got too involved in the writer's history (a counselor's job) and lost track of the reason the writer came in—to work on a specific project.

Overwhelming a writer is the second category of unproductive over sessions. Here, the tutor, trying to be thorough, gives the writer too much information to process. The writer wants to thoroughly revise a fifteen-page paper. As the writer reads the paper, the tutor stops to point out sentence level concerns in every other sentence. With the tutor's help, the writer revises passive voice, repairs focus problems, sorts out commas, and corrects citations. After 30 minutes, the writer's voice has gone flat. The writer stops reading, looks up wearily, and thanks the tutor for the time. "I will finish it on my own." The tutor buried the writer in too much information. Instead of picking just a few things to talk about, the tutor left the writer with the impression that there was just too much to do in the paper. With so much advice, the writer grew disheartened, and the session flopped.

On occasion, tutors cross the line by *taking over* a session. For example, a writer wishes to turn a paper on Anasazi archeological sites in the Four Corners area into a proposal for an independent study. The tutor finds this to be an interesting prospect and is genuinely curious about the Anasazi. What might otherwise seem like a perfect setup for a great session becomes unproductive as the tutor makes the project too much his or her own. Lines like, "Let me see if I can figure this out," "What do you think of rearranging this section like this?" and "I like this word better, don't you?" reveal that the tutor is fully engaged in his or her own thinking about the writing project. The writer withdraws a bit and lets the tutor do the work. The writer might be happy with the well-constructed and well-edited result of such a session but he or she did not learn more about becoming a good writer. In terms of tutoring, the session was unproductive.

There are several ways to cross the line between a productive tutorial where the writer learns about drafting, revising, editing, or some combination of the three, and an unproductive session where the writer gains little to carry into the next writing project. What can a tutor do to recognize the line and return to a productive session?

Getting Back on Safe Ground

My rule of thumb is this: If you think you have stepped over the line, you probably have. When a tutor senses that the session is not going as well as it might, the tutor should reevaluate his or her role in the session. Hallmarks of having overstepped the tutor role include talking more than the writer, noticing that the writer appears distracted or uninterested, and finding that the writer is always choosing the tutor's suggestions. Or, you know you've overstepped if you feel tired at the end of the session while the writer looks refreshed. Body language gives clues, too. If the writer is not leaning in toward the paper, then she is probably not engaged. Eye contact is another sign. As you look into the writer's eyes, do you see boredom, frustration, anger? The crossed line may be clear from across the room at this point.

Having crossed into unproductivity, tutors can get themselves back on track. First they must stop whatever it is that has made the session unproductive. Quit talking, listening, doing, or suggesting in the way that is problematic. A tutor can even remark on this change. "Gee, I seem to have gotten carried away," "You know, I forgot to ask you to make these changes. Please look at the next sentence," or "Let's get to the business of the paper, okay?" Experience teaches tutors that it is possible to recover from line crossings and to move on.

To recover from overempathizing, tutors must remember that counseling is not their major role. Some tutors, especially those trained to work in residence halls, are better equipped than others to talk about personal problems and to know when they are in past their depth. Writing tutors generally do not have such training. Even if it seems a little rude, writing tutors must disclaim any ability to counsel. Although, as Muriel Harris points out (this volume), tutors can benefit from learning to use some of the conversational strategies that professional counselors use. A tutor can suggest some of the resources available on campus for stress management, study skills training, and so on. The writing center director can also provide guidance, especially when the tutor is concerned for the writer's well-being.

For tutors who might be concerned about overwhelming a writer or taking over a session, a technique suggested and used by a peer tutor at Colorado College can help. At the end of every paragraph or so, Amy Weible asks the writer how he or she feels about the changes they have made. This creates opportunities to change course in case the writer is uneasy with the progress of the session. Asking the writer about his or her feelings also helps to remind the tutor whose paper it is and who should be setting the pace and direction of the session. Especially whenever I feel a writer withdraw from the activity of the session, I ask, "Is this what you want to be doing?" or "Is this what you had in mind for your paper?" Writers sometimes apologize for thinking about something else or explain that they really do not have the energy for a full scale, sentence-by-sentence revision after all. Instead of continuing on my path and taking over the session or overwhelming the writer, I can easily redirect my energies and follow the writer's lead. The session can return to being productive.

Complicating Matters

While the advice I offer works in the cases I cited, experienced tutors know that no two sessions are alike. The safe ground of one session is quicksand in another. Some writers delight in having a real person to talk with about their ideas. They have formed their own opinions and are unlikely to be easily swayed by anyone's suggestions. They carefully consider each change to a paper, making sure it is their own change. How different from the writer who is thrown into a tizzy when a tutor starts asking questions about the assumptions of a project or even to have technical jargon explained. They are no longer sure of anything about their paper. They take every question about content to be a weakness with the paper. The tutor must be alert to the writer's reactions to the session.

It is not exactly reassuring to realize that the line always moves and that tutors find it by crossing it. Tutors have to take chances, however. Being too cautious results in sessions that are dull and unproductive. Writers come to the writing center to move their projects along; what a shame to lose them because the tutors try too hard to stay on safe ground. Tutors should not worry about taking chances or making mistakes; we are human, after all. It is normal for someone interested in writing to get excited about ideas. I encourage tutors in our writing center to give themselves a warning when they get really excited about someone else's writing project. Observe the writer's reactions and watch out for the line. Although undoubtedly everyone will misstep a bit, everyone can recover.

As writing centers learn to respond to the needs of international and ethnically diverse populations, crosscultural tutorials can be occasions for plenty of missteps. Some of the advice offered in this chapter may take you in the wrong direction when there are crosscultural misunderstandings at work. This most welcome complication reminds us how important it is for tutors to explain their roles and to ask writers about their expectations for the session. As a writing center director, I'm reminded to include multicultural training in tutor preparation courses, particularly training in recognizing and putting aside generalizations about national and ethnic groups.[6] Each writer is different, each session is new.

Faculty members can add another layer of complication when it comes to crossing the line, especially if they are unaware of the philosophy that informs most tutoring programs. They may be uneasy about the relationship between tutors and writers, concerned about the roles that tutors play and how they help writers, and for reasons discussed earlier, unsure about whose work is being handed in for a grade.[7] Tutoring programs gain the trust of faculty members with productive sessions that are writer- and process-centered. Not crossing the line egregiously maintains that important trust. Without assignments from the faculty, few student writers would have the occasion or the motivation to seek out the writing center. Without support from faculty members, tutoring programs can wither. If tutors routinely cross the line without returning to safe ground, they risk losing the trust of faculty and undermining the entire tutoring program. Luckily, tutors do not routinely cross the line and writing centers work hard to communicate with faculty members.

All these complicating matters have at their base the ideas of collaboration, ethics, and power. As Irene Clark puts it, "In writing labs and centers, . . . the kinds of assistance, which occurs regularly among colleagues, might raise questions, if not eyebrows, over issues of ethics."[8] The academy places different standards of acceptable collaboration on teachers, colleagues, tutors, and classmates. When an individual plays two or three of these roles, working with writers gets complicated. Debating whether these different standards are fair or even useful is a valuable part of any tutor's training. The debate hinges on questions of authority and power. For tutors, the questions about a particular session are many. Did the session diminish the writer's authority? Did the writer make all the decisions about the paper? Who directed the session? Who was in charge of the agenda? Was it a productive session? Did the writer learn something about writing that can be used in the next writing project? These perennial questions are at the base of any tutoring program. The answers point to how productive a session—and how successful a tutoring program—you have co-created.

Further Reading

Clark, Irene Lurkis. 1988. "Collaboration and Ethics in Writing Center Pedagogy." *Writing Center Journal* 9 (1): 3–12.

Clark discusses the many ethical concerns that have arisen around writing center tutoring, especially plagiarism. While agreeing that tutors should never do the bulk of the work, Clark points out that there are occasions when proofreading and editing can be instructive and ethical. She argues that tutors must be encouraged to be flexible about the help they provide writers.

Severino, Carol. 1992. "Rhetorically Analyzing Collaboration(s)." *Writing Center Journal.* 13 (1): 53–64.

Severino provides a set of situational and interpersonal features to look at when analyzing the dynamics of a peer tutoring session. She then analyzes tutorial sessions using these features determining "how much a peer and how much a tutor a peer tutor is." Among other things, such analysis helps tutors determine when to shift between a directive/hierarchical mode and a nondirective/dialogic mode.

Sherwood, Steve. 1995. "The Dark Side of the Helping Personality: Student Dependency and the Potential for Tutor Burnout." In *Writing Center Perspectives,* eds. B. Stay, C. Murphy and E. Hobson, 63–70. Emmitsburg, MD: National Writing Centers Association Press.

As the title suggests, Sherwood looks at when a tutor's tendency to be helpful can cause real trouble. He lists symptoms of neurotic unselfishness that lead to creating student dependency and other problems for writing centers and the profession. He suggests using detached concern to correct for this martyr complex gone awry.

Notes

1. Stephen North, "The Idea of a Writing Center," *College English* 46 (1984): 438.

2. Toni-Lee Capossela, *The Harcourt Brace Guide to Peer Tutoring* (Fort Worth, TX: Harcourt Brace College Publishers, 1998), 2.

3. Christina Murphy and Steve Sherwood, *The St. Martin's Sourcebook for Writing Tutors* (New York: St. Martin's Press, 1995), 13.

4. Murphy and Sherwood, 15.

5. Leigh Ryan, *The Bedford Guide for Writing Tutors* (Boston: St. Martin's Press, 1994), 23–4.

6. Peter Mulvihill, Keith Nitta, and Molly Wingate, "Into the Fray: Ethnicity and Tutor Preparation," *The Writing Lab Newsletter* 19 (7) (1995): 2.

7. For an example of this, see Steve Sherwood, "Ethics and Improvisation," *The Writing Lab Newsletter* 22 (4) (1997): 1.

8. Irene Lurkis Clark, "Collaboration and Ethics in Writing Center Pedagogy," *The Writing Center Journal* 9 (1) (1988): 3.

Works Cited

Capossela, T. 1998. *The Harcourt Brace Guide to Peer Tutoring*. Fort Worth, TX: Harcourt Brace College Publishers.

Clark, I. L. 1988. "Collaboration and Ethics in Writing Center Pedagogy." *The Writing Center Journal* 9 (1): 3–12.

Mulvihill, P., K. Nitta, and M. Wingate. 1995. "Into the Fray: Ethnicity and Tutor Preparation." *Writing Lab Newsletter* 19 (7): 1–5.

Murphy, C., and S. Sherwood. 1995. *The St. Martin's Sourcebook for Writing Tutors*. New York: St. Martin's Press.

North, S. 1984. "The Idea of a Writing Center." *College English* 46: 433–46.

Ryan, L. 1994. *The Bedford Guide for Writing Tutors*. Boston: St. Martin's Press.

Sherwood, S. 1997. "Ethics and Improvisation." *The Writing Lab Newsletter* 22 (4): 1–5.

3

Tutoring in Emotionally Charged Sessions

Corinne Agostinelli, Helena Poch, and Elizabeth Santoro

Since peer tutoring is an interaction between human beings, each with their own ideas and experiences, the potential for conflict is always present.[1] Perhaps the writer has chosen a subject that is particularly close to his heart, so much so that he is unable to look at the writing objectively. Or perhaps the writer has particularly strong feelings about the subject she has chosen, making it difficult or even impossible for a tutor to work objectively with the writing. Situations like these come up often enough to present real dilemmas that leave us uncertain about what to do. In this chapter we will explore ways to handle emotionally charged sessions and offer different perspectives for thinking about them. As tutors, our primary responsibility is to see that the writer gets the help that he or she needs. We will focus on doing this in a respectful and productive way.

While much has been written about how to tutor, most advice deals with more practical matters such as how to ask thought-provoking questions or how to deal with time constraints. The literature about tutoring tends to focus mostly on the "brain," leaving out the "heart." However, our experiences in the writing center tell us that we need to be prepared for both aspects of tutoring. At least one recent book, Martha Maxwell's *When Tutor Meets Student,* informs our understanding of emotional issues by presenting a collection of stories written by writing tutors about their experiences. A few of these stories address topics such as how to handle sexist or racist writers, what to do when a personal tragedy affects a writer's ability to work, and how to build a trusting relationship between tutor and writer. Occasionally peer tutor newsletters like *The Dangling Modifier* or *The Writing Lab Newsletter* publish pieces about emotional conflict, or the topic is discussed at conferences like the National

---

SEE DISCUSSION TOPIC #1 AT THE END OF THIS BOOK

Conference on Peer Tutoring in Writing, which in 1998 was the impetus for this chapter.[2] For the most part, however, a tutor is expected to figure out the "heart" aspects of tutoring on her own. We've developed through experience our own ways of dealing with sensitive situations.

The following incident illustrates our point. A young woman's instructor gave the assignment, "Tell me about a moment in your life that says something about the rest of your life." She was having difficulty describing to her tutor what her problems with the paper were and elected, instead, to simply dive in and read the paper aloud. Two sentences into it, she choked up and began to weep. It turned out that she had chosen to write about her mother's rape as a teenager, and how hearing that story had made this young woman overly cautious and paranoid when she entered college. Her emotions had blocked her ability to work with the paper; she had, in fact, written a piece that was as confused as she was.

No tutor can be completely prepared for situations like this, but we can begin to imagine how intense feelings can impact a tutorial session and how we might respond most effectively.

What to Do?

When a tutor is faced with a situation involving a traumatic experience the writer had, it is tempting to want to make the writer feel better by responding sympathetically—patting him on the shoulder, sharing a personal experience, or allowing the session to become therapy instead of tutoring. It can be awkward to analyze someone's paper in a professional manner when raw emotions, perhaps some that hit us close to home, inspired its creation. Writers may become defensive or emotional toward our suggestions, unable to step outside the paper and fearful that revising will change its emotional impact.

What is most important in such situations is focus and firmness. We have the complicated responsibility of showing empathy to writers while not allowing them to lose sight of the reason that they came for help in the first place: to express ideas effectively. The problem with emotions, obviously, is that they cloud judgment and rationality on both sides, making for a potentially conflict-filled session. Deep passion for a certain subject or situation can also give otherwise overused topics an entirely new dimension. Imagine a discussion of the adoption process by a woman who surrendered a child when she was eighteen years old, or anti-war sentiments expressed by an ex-marine. When a writer decides to use a personal experience or a deep-seated personal value for an academic paper, it is a tutor's responsibility to help the writer articulate the ideas he has and to provide a fair-minded response, even if it means reaching deep inside ourselves to do so. This point is reinforced in a book by J. A. Kottler, who believes that people who help others can learn a lot about themselves when they have to deal with difficult situations, which may force us to be more flexible, creative, and innovative than we ever thought possible. And they require us to look deep inside ourselves to examine every one of our own unresolved issues that get in the way of our being compassionate and effective—both as professionals and as human beings.[3]

Developing a clear goal with the writer for the session is one means of getting some distance from delicate subject matter. This allows the writer not to have to delve into how he or she feels, and allows the tutor to decide whether she is prepared to give emotional support. While this is an easy suggestion to make, it is difficult and emotionally draining to implement. We are human beings, after all.

In our writing center, we have found the following approaches to be successful in different situations. However, as with all things emotional, each of us has had to experiment to find what is most comfortable and what is appropriate for each new experience.

Acknowledge the difficulty of discussing a personal experience. Whether it is a disclosure of childhood abuse or a commentary on the death of a parent, whether the tutor has had a similar experience or not, it is best to acknowledge rather than ignore the burden of the writer's task. "Congratulations on being able to put this on paper. A lot of people would have a hard time sharing an experience like this," is one way to begin. While this suggestion seems elementary, the writer still needs to hear it. Human beings need to hear that they are being listened to and understood; taking a few minutes to empathize will establish a degree of trust. Now is also the time to remind the writer that tutoring sessions are, in fact, confidential.

Keep pushing the focus that the writer wants to achieve. This is not callous and insensitive when you remember that a tutor is not a therapist; we are limited to offering a tissue, a glass of water, and compassion. Tutors do not have the background or training to offer psychological analysis or counseling. Some would argue that writing itself is the best form of therapy, a theory that tutors probably *do* have the experience to share. (See Harris, this volume.)

Imagine, for example, a writer who arrives with a paper in which she is to describe her hero. She has chosen to write about her stepfather, a man who has been a part of her life since she was a very young child. As she wrestles with her gratitude that he is paying for her college experience, on one hand, and her guilt for loving her stepfather more than her birth father, on the other hand, the tutor is spurred to think about her own father and their close relationship. Through the cloudiness of emotions, though, it is clear that the paper is disorganized and lacks a thesis. The tutor's response might be as follows:

"You're so lucky to have had him there when you were growing up. Does he know that you're writing this about him?" After allowing the writer to answer, the tutor might then respond, "If you were going to let him read this, what would you want him to get from it?"

With this response, the writer is reassured that her emotions are valid; she is also forced to really think about why she is writing—not simply to tell about the nice things that her stepfather has done for her, but to thank him, perhaps, specifically for being a father when her birth father wasn't there.

If all else fails, suggest that the writer may need some more time. He may need to sort out newly surfaced emotions before trying to present them for a graded assignment. Someone who has recently battled a drug problem or whose best friend was just killed in a car accident should probably not force himself to write about it until the time is right. In this case, a tutor can offer to help in brainstorming another, equally suitable topic. Perhaps the writer will be relieved to learn that it's acceptable to put a piece of writing on a shelf for a while and that to do so does not show weakness or denial.

Remember that all tutors hope to achieve the same basic goal: to assist others in expressing the ideas they want to convey. Whether the writer's motivation is driven by ego, emotion, or personal growth, the goal should still be the same.

Complicating Matters

Further complicating the issue of sensitivity in tutoring are the tutor's own emotions and opinions and the writer's (intentional or unintentional) use of insensitive or offensive language in papers.

We live in a multicultural society where differences among people are commonplace, though not always respected. Tutors may also have expectations of people that grow out of their own prejudice, such as the mistaken belief that quiet students are unmotivated or that students in basic writing courses are academically weak. Occasionally our prejudices will reveal themselves, and the offended student we are helping may or may not react. This is one of those awkward, inevitable moments in life we all have to learn to deal with. The important thing for any tutor to remember is really quite simple. The moment you realize you have stereotyped or offended the writer, apologize. Then move on, and try never to do it again. Later, do your part to raise consciousness, and for your next staff meeting invite a speaker from your student affairs office to talk about problems of discrimination on campus and how to overcome them (see also Wingate, this volume).

Inappropriate References for Cultural, Racial, or Ethnic Groups

Sometimes peer tutors are in a unique position to let a writer know, politely but firmly, that he or she has made a racial or ethnic slur. Just about everyone who speaks English knows that there are highly derogatory terms used to refer to African Americans, Native Americans, Asians, Hispanics, Jews, and many other groups. Some, however, are less common: "Gypped" (as in "we had a deal and he gypped me"), for example, is an ethnically derogatory term whose root is the same as that of an itinerant race of people. There are numerous words such as these that are inflammatory and insulting. In addition, tutors need to be prepared to talk to writers about other potentially demeaning references to people, like "Indian" for Native American and "girl" for an adult female. Because many derogatory references are local and regional, you might try exchanging ideas on how to deal with them with other tutors in a Tutor Notebook (see Eckard and Staben, this volume).

In some cases, the use of such terms is innocent in that it did not occur to the writer that the term was offensive. Even if the writer is using the term without malice, the tutor needs to make the writer aware of the offending term. Unless the writer intends to provoke a specific response from the audience, the tutor should tell him that some readers will react negatively to what he has written.

Though negative terms stand out and can be easily eliminated, the kind of stereotyping that can be most detrimental tends to lurk beneath the surface; it usually occurs in what the writer appears to be implying about others. This can be harder to talk about because it is easier for the writer to deny and for the tutor to ignore. If the negative implication is fairly clear, however, the tutor should point it out, not ignore it, because the writer needs to be made aware of the reader's response.

Tutors' Emotions

As if tutoring was not complex enough, tutors may also have to deal with their own emotions regarding a particular topic. Because we exhibit the same human vulnerabilities as the writers with whom we work, we are bound to encounter subject matter that we find offensive, hurtful, or heart-wrenching. Specific examples might include helping a writer with a paper about cancer when the tutor has just lost a loved one to the disease, or tutoring a paper about the immorality of homosexuality when the tutor is a homosexual. What should the tutor do when he or she encounters situations such as these?

Before attempting to help another writer, tutors need to evaluate their own feelings about the sensitive topic. Some questions that tutors might want to ask themselves include: Am I able to be objective with this paper? Are my responses going to be emotionally wrought? Can I separate my feelings about this topic from my professional opinion about the merits and faults of the work?

Often the session may go more smoothly if the tutor is simply honest with the writer about his or her feelings on the topic. The writer can then decide whether or not to continue the session. Consider, for example, a writer who presents a paper in which she colorfully expresses her distaste for the Greek system, and a tutor who happens to be an active member of a fraternity or a sorority. The tutor's response might be, "Now, you say that all the Greeks do is drink beer on the weekends and cause vandalism. Aren't they, historically, philanthropic organizations? Don't most of them, if not all, sponsor charities?"

With this response, the tutor is able to reveal his or her bias while also being devil's advocate as a means to help the writer think about her argument. An opinion paper is nothing, really, if a writer is simply "preaching to the choir," and so part of a tutor's job is to get the writer to consider how this paper might be too simplistic and why he needs to develop a more complete, thoughtful picture. (See Rafoth, this volume.)

There are times in which playing devil's advocate can be inappropriate. If a writer comes to the center with a paper that decries homosexuality and the tutor is a homosexual, this is probably not the best time for the tutor to come out. In cases such as this, if another tutor is available, it would probably be better to switch tutors or have two tutors work together to control emotional responses. If no other tutor is available, then tutors must deal with the situation according to their center's policy.

In all cases, if a tutor feels that his or her personal safety could be threatened as a result of working with a particular writer (as might be the case with a homosexual tutor assisting a homophobic writer), then the police or campus security should be called. While such cases are rare, it is vital that they be discussed in staff meetings or with the director.

In conclusion, for a writer to make the decision to pour his or her emotions onto paper and open those emotions up for a classroom grade shows a tremendous amount of strength. Oftentimes writers will come to the writing center for validation that their topic is important and appropriate, not necessarily for the purpose of receiving help, but still making our jobs that much more challenging.

Like any profession that involves more than one person expressing ideas and discussing experiences, tutoring writing is complicated by the emotional responses of everyone involved. Thinking and planning in advance about how to handle emotional situations can make all the difference in a tutoring session. Although highly sensitive sessions remain the exception and not the rule, dealing with them is part of the essence of what we do as tutors: creating an open, respectful, and productive environment for learning to write.

Further Reading

Daniell, Beth. May 1994. "Composing (as) Power." *College Composition and Communication* 45 (2), 238–46.

Colleges and university professors, and some tutors as well, are not always receptive to students who write about their religious faith. In this article, Daniell argues that it is a mistake to ignore the connection between religion and empowerment, and she observes that spiritual and religious motives throughout history have actually motivated people to seek literacy. It is troubling, she says, when academics dismiss the spiritual and religious aspects of students' lives. Tutors who are interested in nontraditional students and feminist issues may be especially interested in the interviews Daniell conducted with six women about how they use literacy in their spiritual lives.

Maxwell, Martha, ed. 1994. *When Tutor Meets Student.* 2nd ed. Ann Arbor, University of Michigan Press.

This is a collection of 54 diverse and interesting stories written by tutors at UC Berkeley. Their accounts depict life experiences in the writing center on such topics as gender relationships, cultural diversity, plagiarism, and tutor dependency. These stories are told in the tutors' own words and make for great reading.

Payne, Michelle. 2000. *Bodily Discourses: When Students Write About Physical Abuse, Sexual Abuse, and Eating Disorders.* Portsmouth, NH: Boynton/Cook.

This book explores ways in which writing teachers can be most helpful to students writing about these topics.

Notes

1. This point is developed nicely by Steve Sherwood in "Ethics and Improvisation," *Writing Lab Newsletter* 22 (4) (1997): 2.

2. National Conference on Peer Tutoring in Writing, The State University of New York at Plattsburgh, Nov. 6–8, 1998. More information about the NCPTW may be found at http://www.chss.iup.edu/wc/ncptw/

3. J. A. Kottler, *Compassionate Therapy: Working with Difficult Clients* (San Francisco, CA: Jossey-Bass, 1992), xi.

Works Cited

Kottler, J. A. 1992. *Compassionate Therapy: Working with Difficult Clients.* San Francisco, CA: Jossey-Bass.

Sherwood, S. 1997. "Ethics and Improvisation." *Writing Lab Newsletter* 22 (4): 1–5.

4

Talk to Me: Engaging Reluctant Writers

Muriel Harris

Every tutor, no matter how dazzlingly effective he or she is, will meet up with a student who responds—or fails to respond—like the one in this all-too-familiar dialogue:

Tutor: Hi, Alisa, how are you doin' today?

Alisa: (Nods silently and briefly, begins searching in her backpack for her paper, and then settles far back into her seat, hands in her lap.)

Tutor: Were you at the game this weekend? I knew we were going to lose, but it was a good game to watch.

Alisa: (Shakes her head slightly, to indicate she didn't go.)

Tutor: Well, what do you want to work on today?

Alisa: Here's my paper. (Alisa looks down, avoiding eye contact.)

Tutor: Why don't you tell me a bit about it. . . . What your main point is, what the assignment is . . . you know, all that stuff that we'll need to know to work on it.

Alisa: It's about cloning. For my Ethics class. It's due in a couple of days.

Tutor: OK, interesting subject. That's a hot topic, and there's lots to say about it. What do you want to work on?

Alisa: Could you see if it's OK?

Tutor: OK, let's start with the main point. Why don't you just tell me first what your main point is. (Waits while the silence grows and expands around them.) Is cloning ethical? Are there ethical problems we should consider before going ahead? Should scientists try to do it?

SEE DISCUSSION TOPIC #1 AT THE END OF THIS BOOK

Alisa: It's OK, I guess.

Tutor: Are you supposed to discuss the ethical implications? Or argue a point of view? Are you writing to people who think cloning should be stopped? Or to people who think it's important to do, like for possible medical uses?

Alisa: It really doesn't much affect me. I don't know. (Alisa shrugs, slumps farther down in her chair, and stares at the people at the next tutorial table.)

Tutor: Did you have a hard time writing this paper? If so, let's talk about that for a bit.

Alisa: (No response.)

And so it goes with the unresponsive student. You try to coax, nudge, or invite the student to get involved in a discussion about the paper. But the student resists and continues to sit there refusing to make eye contact or lean closer to the table. Nothing seems to engage the writer into the conversation you'd like to have about that paper lying limp and forlorn on the table between you and the student. You recognize the student's sense of being withdrawn from the tutorial by the student's body language, voice tone, the long silences that meet your attempts to chat, the monosyllables that pass as answers, and the shrugs that follow.

Some Background

The reasons for students' unresponsive behavior range widely, and clues as to why a student is not responding to the tutor's efforts are usually inadequate. Some possibilities to consider:

- *The student is forced to be there.*

When we are required to do something, some people react negatively. They may blame whoever required their attendance or whomever they meet in the process of fulfilling what was required of them. Psychologists who prepare therapists and counselors explain that it's not unusual for clients to become angry at whomever they have to meet with, even if that person is not involved in setting the requirement. Similarly, when an unwilling student is assigned to come to the writing center, the student is likely to resist a tutor's overtures to engage in any conversation. She doesn't want to be there and hopes to be able to leave as soon as possible.

- *Writing is not important to this writer.*

Writing is seen by some students (usually mistakenly, but they don't learn this until they graduate and have to communicate on the job) as a requirement that has little to do with their lives. They envision themselves as engineers in design labs, as programmers of the next generation of cool software, as pharmacists or farmers who will be far from the world of reports and memos. They assume that the business world proceeds via cell phones, not written memos or letters (which, if needed, secretaries will clean up). And, finally, they see no need for a tutor's help with writing any more than they would attend closely to someone explaining how to build mud huts. It's simply not relevant to their lives, and they most likely came to the writing center because it was required, because they thought they'd earn extra points with the teacher, or because they want the tutor to fix the paper so they can get a higher grade.

- ***The writer may be anxious about revealing ignorance or poor writing to anyone and nervous about being critiqued.***

For a study I conducted to learn about students' concerns in writing tutorials ("Talking in the Middle"), I read hundreds of student responses on anonymous evaluations filled out at the end of tutorials in our Writing Lab. Over and over, they commented how relieved they were that they weren't "slammed" or "laughed at" or "ripped" by the tutor. They were surprised that the tutor didn't talk down to them. They announced that the tutorial was successful because they now felt more confident, though it was usually not clear if they meant more confident about themselves or their writing — or perhaps both. From comments like these, we become more aware of how apprehensive students are when they come to writing centers. Under such emotional strains, they may be very likely to shut up, to wonder what they're supposed to do, and finally, to be as unengaged as any tutor might be in a strange situation. When we have no idea what's expected of us and we feel shaky about whether we are going to be ridiculed or asked to demonstrate what we don't know, we do sometimes respond by withdrawing until we can get a better handle on what's happening or figure out how we can retreat from the situation with minimal embarrassment.

- ***The student is overwhelmed by other concerns.***

The student who doesn't want to engage in tutorial conversation may have just heard that he's running out of student financial aid, that there was a major quiz in the chem lecture he missed, or that his girlfriend has dumped him. Students bring with them a variety of other problems and worries and disappointments that affect their ability (or inability) to attend to what's going on in the writing tutorial. Issues that can affect students' writing are categorized by Leigh Ryan as academic (grades, study skills, test anxiety), social (separation from family and friends, peer pressure, roommates), and lifestyle (finances, independence, job responsibilities).[1]

- ***The writer doesn't have the language to talk about his or her writing.***

Researchers on cognitive processes involved in writing and revising (Flower, et al.) have explained that like other problem-solving tasks, effective revision requires the ability to detect problems in the draft of a paper and to find strategies to use to solve those problems. Without such abilities, which are often lacking in beginning writers, they don't know how to explain to someone else what they want to work on or what their problem is. Such students are likely to come in flustered, ill-at-ease, and unable to say more than "my paper's too short," "the paper doesn't flow," or "I just don't like it," or "it's not what I wanted to say" and hope that the tutor somehow understands what they mean. They lapse into silence because they don't know what to say or how to say it. Like the patient in a doctor's office, they hope that by sitting quietly while the doctor examines them, the doctor will diagnose their problem and prescribe a treatment.

- ### *The writer is simply a very quiet person.*

Much research on personality type has helped us to define personality preferences, those ways of interacting with the world that are neither right nor wrong, simply ways that people differ. The Myers-Briggs Type Indicator (MBTI), one of the most useful and most well-researched ways to sort out personality preferences, has stimulated a great deal of research on how personality types interact with writing and tutoring. A particularly helpful collection of essays about this is Thomas C. Thompson's *Most Excellent Differences: Using Type Theory in the Composition Classroom.* In the introduction to type theory Thompson defines one of the MBTI dimensions as Extraversion and Introversion, noting that introverts prefer to "play out potential actions mentally before deciding whether they actually wanted to follow through with them."[2] A further picture of how introverts prefer to deal with the world shows us how we might interpret their unresponsiveness as not being engaged when, in fact, they are simply taking things in to reflect on them quietly—on their own at a later time. Here's Thompson's picture:

> Because [introverts] like to rehearse their answers before speaking, they may
> be slow to respond to questions about new material. Introverts often choose
> to sit near the edge of the classroom, where they can observe class activities
> without being caught in the middle of them.[3]

And, of course, some people are just naturally shy or quiet, not given to a lot of chatter. Some of us love to pour out words; others use them sparingly. Some find silence in a conversation awkward; others appreciate it as time for reflection.

- ### *The student knows that if he or she shuts up, the tutor (or teacher) will do all the work.*

Some students who have been in school for a number of years learn how to play the teacher/tutor game to their advantage. In lectures, large classrooms, and even small ones, they've learned that they are expected to shut up, be passive, and wait for the teacher to answer her own questions. This role is all too familiar. Less familiar is the one that tutors are trying to get the student to play— to be active learners who take charge of their own learning. So they wait for the tutor to tell them what to write, how to fix the paper, or maybe—if they sit quietly long enough—even do the rewriting.

What to Do

While it's not always clear which of the possibilities listed above looms largest in keeping the student withdrawn from the situation, here are some strategies to try:

- *Empathize about being forced to do something.*

When you ask the student if her visit is required and she indicates morosely that she's there because she has to be and her actions indicate that she has no interest in doing anything much beyond sitting there until the time is up and she can leave, you can try talking openly and honestly about her not wanting to be there. Empathize, let her know that you too have been in situations you were forced into and that you too felt as she does. After all, it isn't the worst trait in the world to be an independent person who isn't exactly pleased when others tell them what to do. Try to help the student see that as long as he's bothered to come to the lab, you'd like to help him make good use of his time. If your center sends notes to teachers, explain—after you've managed to get the student to see that you are interested in his welfare—that you have to report on what was worked on and if nothing was talked about, the teacher isn't likely to consider the requirement fulfilled. Have the student help you write the note (or let him write it himself). If none of this mobilizes the student into some minimal conversation, you have probably done what you could. You need to let the student leave, but you've warned him (in friendly terms) that sitting there won't satisfy the instructor. Just as we encourage students to make their own decisions about what they want to write, letting them make the decision to leave without really satisfying the requirement at least keeps students in the driver's seat. Some tutors find that these students return later, on their own, when it's not required and after they've realized that tutors aren't there to force them to do anything.

- *Acknowledge the lack of interest in writing and try for a small success.*

For writers who admit that they have little interest in writing and say that it isn't relevant to them, you can start by acknowledging this attitude as something many students share. But then try talking about when the student might need writing skills—in classes (exams, reports) or for that person's career (job applications, memos). Harold Hackney and Sherilyn Cormier, in their book on how counselors can help clients, warn us that "unless clients can determine some personal goals for counseling, the probability of change is minimal."[4] You won't win over everyone because some students will remain unconvinced that being a better writer is a personal goal of theirs, and they will continue to expend as little effort as possible. Then, it's time to try for a minimal bit of success. The student has some piece of writing to work on or she wouldn't be there. What can be done with that one paper? One tutor in our Writing Lab, when backed into such corners by students who merely wanted to pass the course and not worry about writing any more, would explain that he realized the student's time was valuable and didn't want to waste it. What could they do together in the few remaining minutes of the tutorial to make it useful for the student? Sometimes that might result in little more than helping the student set up his two citations in MLA format or learn the difference between "it's" and "its," but at least the time together was not a total waste.

- *Help the student talk about his or her fears.*

If you sense the student is quiet because he is overcome by anxiety or fears of some kind related to meeting you and talking about his writing, try to establish an atmosphere of trust, perhaps by being friendly, by explaining that you're not a teacher and that your job is to help and to listen. Then invite the student to talk about his or her anxieties. In their suggestions to counselors who work with fearful clients, psychotherapists Randolph Pipes and Donna Davenport (see Further Reading) tell us that such clients often cannot overcome their resistance to getting involved until the underlying fears are expressed. Then, it is important to empathize and to reassure the student that such fears are not uncommon and can be overcome. The core of such a conversation might sound like this:

Tutor: You don't seem to want to talk about your paper. Would you like me to read it instead, or would that bother you? When I was in freshman comp, I hated having my paper read by anyone, especially out loud in class and in front of others. I wouldn't even let my roommate read my papers.

Writer: I'm not a good writer. My teachers hate my writing. I'll never be good at it.

Tutor: I honestly don't know a whole lot of people who think they're great writers. Writing takes work, and you probably aren't happy with what you write. That's pretty usual. And we can work on your writing together. I bet there's lots of good stuff here to work with.

Writer: I hate when someone criticizes my writing. I won't show it to anyone except my teacher.

Tutor: Hey, I'm not going to criticize. Really. My job is to help you. In fact, I like the first paragraph here, especially when you start out with that good question in your first sentence. Talking about your writing with someone else usually helps a lot.

- *Reschedule for a better time or listen and move on.*

For students who seem withdrawn or remain unengaged because there might be other, more pressing problems on their minds, you can ask if they want to come back some other time. Or if the student starts to talk about what's worrying her, listen. Give the student a few minutes to vent or explain what's really on her mind, and really listen. Pipes and Davenport distinguish between "social listening," which is often largely a matter of not interrupting, maybe nodding from time to time, or thinking of what you're going to say next, and "therapeutic listening," which requires much more. The therapeutic listener attends closely, really hears what the client is saying and both processes cognitively what the client is saying while empathizing closely with what is being said. A few minutes of such conversation is likely to help clear the air, but if you sense that the person starts bringing up other problems, having found a listening ear, it's probably clear that the student is deciding to use the time as a support session for his life, his troubles, his frustration with his roommate. One strategy to get back to work is first to acknowledge that you've heard the student and that it's time to move on. You can show that you were listening by reflecting back to the student what she said: "Yeah, getting a speeding ticket really upsets you. But now let's focus on something positive, like getting that paper revised." Or "You sound like you're fearful about what's happening with your mom, but I'm not trained to help you with that. There's a good psych services here on campus. It's free, and a couple of my friends went there and were glad they did. I can help you make an appointment. But, for now, since we only have about 20 minutes left, what can we do in that time to help you revise this paper?"

- *Offer the student some questions she can ask herself.*

When a student can't offer much beyond general unease about the paper (not liking it, thinking it doesn't flow, etc.) and you suspect that the student is quiet because he has nothing else to say, try giving the student some possible questions to ask himself:

> "Could you tell me if part of the problem is that what you wanted to do in this paper—what's in your head—doesn't match with what's here on the page?"
> (or)
> "Do you think the lack of flow is because there aren't words to tie the sentences and paragraphs together? Or maybe you think it doesn't flow because it jumps from topic to topic? Sometimes, people get that 'lack of flow' feeling when the order is jumbled or when they're not sure whether the different parts are in some kind of logical order?"
> (or)
> "Are you wondering if the paper doesn't meet the assignment? Or the kind of paper it's supposed to be, like a persuasion paper or a definition paper?"

If this helps the student to start talking, you can remind him that these are good questions to ask himself when he's working on a draft and wants to improve it. You may have to keep listing questions and problems the student's paper might have until something strikes a responsive chord. When he hears something that begins to sound right, he will begin—probably hesitantly—to talk more easily about what he wants to work on.

- *Give the student some quiet time to think and write.*

If you meet up with a truly quiet person who has little to say, you don't have to fill the silence with talk. Let that person process what is being said and leave some quiet time for her to think about your question. Ask if she'd prefer to try writing about it herself while you work with another student, assuring her that you'll come back to continue working together. Try to set a specific task for her to work on:

Tutor: "If you're having difficulties making the paper longer, why not try the journalist's questions—who, what, where, why, when, how? Maybe who's going to benefit from more student parking on campus; where such parking would be; why the administration should consider your proposal; what the administration might bring up as arguments against your proposal. Want to write down those question words to think about? I'll be back in awhile to see how you're doing, OK?

In their discussion of how to use personality preferences to work with writing, Sharon Cramer and Tom Reigstad found that for those who score highly as extraverts on the MBTI scale "an opportunity to brainstorm with fellow writers would be welcome [while] . . . individuals with the 'introverted' preference . . . would more likely benefit from independent brooding in private and would write best in a sanctuary, like a study carrel."[5]

  • ***Try minimalist tutoring.***

When the writer keeps looking to you to do all the work and is willing to sit there silently and out-wait you, you can try Jeff Brooks' "defensive minimalist tutoring." Drawing on his experience in tutoring such students, he recommends mimicking the student's body language. If the student slouches back in his chair, getting as far away as possible, the tutor can also physically move away, also slouching back into her chair. Jane Wilson, another tutor who has encountered such students, seconds this strategy: "If the student acts tired out and disinterested, the tutor can lay back in his chair and wait for something to happen. In this case, the pressure is now on the student to do something."[6] Even if being a defensive minimalist tutor is not your style, too over the top for you, try to ask questions that indicate you are interested in the student's answers, refrain from answering your own questions, and give the student plenty of wait time to answer. Eventually, most students get involved, at least minimally.

Complicating Matters

The strategies offered here come with a number of caveats. They may not work, but if they do, they may work in ways you don't want them to. For example, if you are successful in helping a writer talk through her fears or anxieties, she may become overly dependent on you. You begin to suspect that some of her visits to the center are mainly to talk with you as a comforting listening ear or to have you look over the paper because she has come to depend on you to approve every paper before handing it in. Then, you have to think about how to help her become independent. It's also possible that by talking to you, the writer is not seeking the kinds of professional help she ought to be getting. You can prepare for this by learning more about the professional resources on your campus. Perhaps professionals from those services can visit your staff meetings and help you to recognize symptoms. Similarly, if you are successful in turning to off-topic conversation, you may find it hard to get the student back to work. By offering an escape valve for what he doesn't want to do, you may have let him continue to avoid working on his writing. His teacher will be equally disappointed, especially if the teacher hears that he went to see a tutor and had a good discussion about changing his major. The teacher will be less likely to refer students to a place where the required work wasn't done. This is also a possible outcome when you tried and tried to get the writer to become engaged in a tutorial and finally had to let him go because he wouldn't or couldn't focus on his writing. Teachers who aren't familiar with tutorial principles and assume the tutor will take control of the session and tell the student what he needs to know will consider the tutor—and the writing center—ineffective.

It would make tutoring much easier if the strategies I've listed above came with a guarantee that they will work. They don't. Every student is a different human being, and as we all know, we all act differently at different times. Moreover, your tutoring style differs from other tutors'. You may be able to be a minimalist tutor, but you may also not find that a comfortable stance because it strikes you as rude. You may welcome students' personal conversations about their lives and problems, or you may be the kind of person for whom this is awkward. While you know that others on your staff can try these counseling strategies, you recognize that you can't. And some days you start off eager to help, and by the end of your assigned time, you really are exhausted and can't listen as closely as you know you want to. So, while strategies sound useful and easy, they aren't recipes. Sometimes the best we can hope for is a repertoire of strategies to draw upon. When one doesn't seem to be working or doesn't fit the way we tutor, we move on to another one. That's what makes tutoring so challenging and finally, when we're successful, so rewarding. In the Writing Lab I work in, we agree that when you've had a bad tutorial, you should try to reflect on what went wrong and learn from it. When you conclude that part of the problem was the student and there's nothing more you can do, let it go. When you've just had a great tutorial, take a moment to just sit and enjoy the feeling.

Further Reading

Bolander, Becky, and Marcia Harrington. 1996. "Reflectivity: Finding Gold in the Crevices of Tutorials." *Writing Lab Newsletter* 20 (10): 1–5.

The authors of this article note that when a student begins to talk about other problems or frustrations in her life, and when tutors listen attentively, valuable information and insights (the gold in the crevices) about the student and her writing can emerge. Bolander and Harrington explain that such listening helps to remind us that students come to tutorials with experiences that affect their writing.

Parbst, John R. 1994. "Off-topic Conversation and the Tutoring Session." *Writing Lab Newsletter* 19 (1): 1–2, 6.

When meeting with a nervous or shy student, John Parbst recommends that tutors try moving away from a tutorial agenda to off-topic conversation. This can result in relaxing the student and, as a side-benefit, may turn up ideas for writing. Possible clues that Parbst suggests for starting off-topic conversation include a student's name that might lead to conversation about the origins of the name and further conversation about the student's background; a student's athletic clothes or sport logos that may lead to questions about the upcoming sports season; or books in a student's backpack that can lead to conversations about other courses or the student's major and future plans.

Pipes, Randolph B., and Donna S. Davenport. 1990. *Introduction to Psychotherapy: Common Clinical Wisdom.* Englewood Cliffs, NJ: Prentice Hall.

Because tutors encounter similar problems that therapists or counselors meet with, this book offers suggestions for tutors as well. Topics include fears counselors have, such as the fear of looking foolish and the fear of not being competent to help; fears that clients may have that will influence how clients act; ways to start the first session; levels of listening and signals of poor listening; methods to deal with the client's resistance to help that is being offered; and so on.

Notes

1. Leigh Ryan, *The Bedford Guide for Writing Tutors* (Boston: Bedford Books of St. Martin's Press, 1994), 48.

2. Thomas C. Thompson, ed., *Most Excellent Differences: Essays in Using Type Theory in the Composition Classroom* (Gainsville: CAPT, 1996), 5.

3. Thompson, 6.

4. Harold L. Hackney and L. Sherilyn Cormier, *The Professional Counselor: A Process Guide to Helping,* 3rd ed. (Boston: Allyn & Bacon, 1996), 117.

5. Sharon Cramer and Tom Reigstad, "Using Personality to Teach Writing," *Composition Chronicle* 7 (2) (March 1994): 4.

6. Jane C. Wilson, "Making the Sale: Helping Students to 'Buy' Writing Skills," *Writing Lab Newsletter* 21 (10) (1999): 13.

Works Cited

Brooks, J. 1991. "Minimalist Tutoring: Making the Student Do All the Work." *Writing Lab Newsletter* 15 (6): 1–4.

Cramer, S., and T. Reigstad. March 1994. "Using Personality to Teach Writing." *Composition Chronicle* 7 (2): 4–7.

Flower, L. R., J. R. Hayes, L. Carey, K. Schriver, and J. Stratman. February 1986. "Detection, Diagnosis, and the Strategies of Revision." *College Composition and Communication* 37: 16–55.

Hackney, H. L., and L. S. Cormier. 1996. *The Professional Counselor: A Process Guide to Helping.* 3rd ed. Boston: Allyn & Bacon.

Harris, M. 1995. "Talking in the Middle: Why Writers Need Writing Tutors." *College English* 57 (1): 27–42.

Ryan, L. 1994. *The Bedford Guide for Writing Tutors.* Boston: Bedford Books of St. Martin's Press.

Thompson, T. C., ed. 1996. *Most Excellent Differences: Essays in Using Type Theory in the Composition Classroom.* Gainsville: CAPT.

Wilson, J. C. 1999. "Making the Sale: Helping Students to 'Buy' Writing Skills." *Writing Lab Newsletter* 21 (10): 13–14.

5

Telling Tutor Tales

Breaking Down Barriers with Stories

Sandra J. Eckard

The silence is deafening despite the sounds I know are present: the muted conversations between tutors and writers, the hum of the lights, the rhythmic tapping of computer keys. Yet all I hear is silence that hangs between us.

I've asked him to tell me what he notices about this passage; he says he knows what's wrong but doesn't know how to fix it.

We are at an impasse, facing an invisible yet impenetrable wall between us.

I take a deep breath, smile, and try something else. We need to find another space—one that is safe, comfortable, a space we can share. "You know, transitions are always difficult for me, too. I have tons of ideas swimming around, yet when I try to get them all down on paper, they sometimes don't seem to go together or say what I want them to. Do you know what I mean?"

He nods and smiles. There has been a subtle, positive change.

This situation—writer and a tutor at a standstill—happens every day in our writing centers. What can we do when other tutoring strategies fail to break through the wall that stands between you? One option, much like my beginning narrative, is telling a story. Although the concept of story may have you envisioning pajamas and the refrain "Once upon a time," storytelling may be found in many tutoring sessions. Between the words on the page and the talk of revision, a different type of exchange can occur, a story of life or experience. "When I was in Freshman Composition . . . " or "Like you, I always have to watch for . . . " have replaced "Once upon a time," but they are transitions into stories nonetheless. Though overlooked, stories can create a positive tutoring environment when things seem to be going nowhere.

SEE DISCUSSION TOPIC **#1** AT THE END OF THIS BOOK

Tutor stories can be elaborate narratives that recount events with plots and characters, like the fables we associate with those "Once upon a time" beginnings. There are other types of stories, however—stories that are crisp and brief. What's common among these stories—whether autobiographical (stories about yourself), memoir (stories about others), or fictive (fictional stories)—is the sprinkle of life, a moment of sharing that connects teller and listener in a space without walls. For whatever reason, some students have great difficulty communicating in a tutoring session, while we tutors can talk of writing, rules, and styles until we are breathless and our writers are numb. This writing talk may create a gulf between writer and tutor rather than bringing them closer together. What is to be done when students don't see the point of working further on their writing? Will our exercises or labels remain with the writer after the tutoring session? For the next paper? If there are walls to tear down between a tutor and a writer, then storytelling may be the answer.

Some Background

In medieval times, stained glass told some of the first stories; craftspeople created images that represented the stories of the Bible. Oral storytelling was also one of the most prominent, and respected, forms of communication. Without the technology we now take for granted—from chalkboards to textbooks to laptops—the story was the primary source for distributing information and, as with stained glass, dispensing religion. As one storytelling researcher writes, " . . . English romances are rarely 'single narrative'; rather they are collections of related versions, versions that may not have been directed at the same audiences or transmitted in the same way."[1] In other words, both the stories and the way we tell them affect the audience. In "Why Tell Stories?" Brian Ellis writes, "In every storytelling experience there is speaking and listening, and motivation for reading and writing."[2] Telling stories, then, can inspire an audience.

Stories can serve another purpose: connection. Tutoring is a personal, one-to-one interaction that involves not only the paper at hand but the participants as well. Richard Meyer writes, "Stories bind a culture or groups of people. . . . Stories do seem to cross boundaries as a way of teaching, learning, remembering, making sense of things, understanding what happens to us, and even predicting what will."[3] In short, stories can help us do more than establish—and maintain—a connection with student writers; they can also make this connection memorable: "A personal story is rarely forgotten because the teller has lived through the experience . . . [providing] a revelation for the listener."[4]

My own experience in writing centers has shown me how important sharing can be in creating safe spaces to talk about writing. I've learned that tutoring involves sharing not only writing, it can also—and usually does—involve serving up a part of our lives along with the requested dish of writing tips. Murphy and Sherwood sum up the tutoring process as contextual, collaborative, interpersonal, and individualized,[5] showing that there are many facets of the tutoring relationship. To put it another way, tutoring is messy; it requires attention, patience, and understanding not only to deal with paper assignments and writing concerns but also with students' confusion and reluctance. Writers don't have to struggle with these obstacles alone, however, as Pam Farrell reminds us: "Writing no longer has to be an isolated activity. Writing is communication and collaboration. The writing lab . . . allows the students to participate in creating ties with the world around them."[6]

Stories, short or long, simple or elaborate, are one way tutors and students can break down walls and open lines of communication by creating a nonthreatening space to talk about ourselves and our writing. Stories do not always succeed in overcoming barriers and they may have unintended consequences—more on this in the final section of this chapter—but they have the potential to work effectively.

What to Do

There are no right or wrong stories, just stories that are appropriate for the goal of overcoming barriers to communication. We each have a wealth of experiences, interests, and memories that we can call upon to tell stories, but as with any tutoring strategy, we need to use them appropriately. Here are some questions to consider when deciding whether to tell a story:

- What do I know about the student as both a writer and a person?
- What options do I have for getting my message across?
- Will my story create a safe space?
- What do I want my story to help the writer think about?

As with all tutoring, you will be asking and answering these questions almost instantly, for tutoring is very much a spontaneous exchange. When writers don't—or can't—open up and discuss how to rethink their writing, stories can expand the room for discussion, allowing writers to enter the conversation and move beyond the walls that prevent them from talking about their writing.

What Types of Stories Can I Use?

The tales that tutors can draw upon can be autobiographical, memoir, or fictive stories that we select in order to achieve our primary goal: helping writers move beyond their apprehensions or lack of experience to begin a dialogue about how, and perhaps why, to rethink their writing.

I'll begin this section on types of stories with an opening narrative that has three possible story endings, A, B, and C, much like one of those choose-your-own-adventure books we read when we were young. This particular adventure,

Nancy and the Case of the Missing Data, portrays a tutoring session where a tutor meets a writer who doesn't immediately embrace the concept of revision. The three endings focus on how the idea of story can be used successfully in tutorial sessions. Each of the possible endings illustrates how autobiographical, memoir, and fictive stories help to bridge the gap between tutor and writer differently.

Nancy and the Case of the Missing Data

She sits silently, yet her posture speaks volumes to me. Arms crossed, body not touching the table, no pen or paper in sight. I can feel her eyes staring holes in me, almost daring me to say anything that begins with the "r" word: revision. Gee, I think, it's hard to be enthusiastic when she doesn't express even a drop of interest.

We finish reading her paper together, and I notice several places that need more research, development of her argument, and examples. Well, it's not going to be easy, but I have something to work with. I think.

"It says here that the final draft must be five typed pages. What else did you like about the book that we could add? Would you like to brainstorm together?"

My questions draw a sigh worthy of Scarlett O'Hara.

I try again. "What about outside resources . . . let's see . . . you need a minimum of how many?"

"It says five, but all the rest of the books were already checked out."

I've heard this before. But okay. Think, Sandy. "Why don't we look at your other paragraphs and ideas? Maybe if we look at each one, we could find something to expand on?"

I see a slight crack in her mask. Minor, and quickly overtaken by indifference, but I saw it. "Why don't we look at the first page, Nancy." I can only help if you let me, I say to myself.

"The prof is always droning on and on about drafting, but I'm not into that."

Suddenly, the problem becomes clear. We are on two different sides of the fence. Her concept of writing is very different from mine. How do we overcome this barrier of understanding? How will I ask her to consider revision? To think about adding research? I gulp and wonder how not to meet the uncool fate of droning on and on.

Ending A: Autobiographical stories about life experiences   We each know our world by our own collection of experiences; we store snapshots and moments that help us understand our lives. As this ending shows, these moments provide analogies that can help in tutoring. . . .

"Well," I begin, clearing my throat. "I often have trouble with, you know, telling everything that I should. I wrote a paper on dolphins and language one time, and when I got my paper back, I was stunned by my grade. Looking at the questions that the professor asked me about my ideas, I realized I had intended to answer all of them, but in between thinking and drafting, all of the connections didn't make it to the paper. I've learned since then that I have a habit of doing that, actually." I grin and pray. I hope a glimpse of Sandy-the-writer will help her see that revision doesn't come easily to me either. It has a price.

"A habit of what?" She is talking to me, even sounding a bit interested. I continue, trying not to look excited. "Hmmm . . . it's like I know what I want to say, but I assume that my words speak for themselves. That my reader will know everything that I'm thinking by the ink on the page."

Silence again. Then, "And?"

"I started reading paragraphs separately, thinking to myself, 'If all I read is this one section, does it say everything I wanted it to say about my topic?'"

I smile and add after a beat, "We could try that if you like."

Nancy doesn't actually say yes, but she moves closer to the table. And that's good enough for me at this point.

Ending B: Memoir—Stories of others' lives and experiences   Memoirs can be influential in breaking down barriers, especially in discussions of revision, as this ending reveals. This type of story can help show writers the composing process through others' adventures (or misadventures) . . .

"Well," I say, "Can I ask you a question?" I don't really pause for an answer, hoping for the best. "How many drafts did you make of this paper before you brought it here to talk with me?"

Nancy looks at me as though I've grown a second head. "One. I did fix some spelling, you know."

"That's a good start. We often write more than one draft. Like with your first: you took some time away from it, went back, and found some spots where you wanted to fix things. Right?" Okay, she didn't do a second draft and I'm exaggerating, but I give her credit anyhow.

She's nodding.

"Most every really good writer does that—revision. It's what writing is all about: looking at the words again to make sure you've put on paper all the thoughts you possibly can. I know of famous writers, even, that spend hours rethinking, reorganizing, even scrapping part, or all, of what they've written. All that time at the computer. Poof. Gone."

This time she nods emphatically. "See," I add, "you know because revising is hard. Thinking about all these writing things, like word choice, imagery, number of resources, options for crafting a draft that is vivid and powerful—that's complicated. Did you know that Ernest Hemingway rewrote the ending to *A Farewell to Arms* thirty-nine times before he was satisfied? Can you imagine him just pulling that paper out of the typewriter and tossing it in the wastepaper can?"

We laugh together.

"But he did it, " I add softly after the laughter fades. "Would you like to look at this draft again with me to see where we could make it even better?"

"Well, I'm not doing it thirty-nine times." There's sarcasm lacing her tone, but I could swear I hear humor as well, and maybe even a bit of enthusiasm, too.

Ending C: Fictive stories about television, movies, or literature   This type of story is equally powerful, but the success of these stories depends greatly on the personality and interests of both the tutor and the tutee. If I analyzed my own storytelling, I would argue that I tell more fictive stories than any other, in all kinds of settings, including the writing center. When possible, I can make some connection to my favorites such as *The X-Files, Buffy the Vampire Slayer,* or *Star Wars* to help make my point. Tutors can use popular culture to connect with writers and find a common ground. As with any tutoring technique, however, we each use it differently. The power lies in selecting what is meaningful to us and the writers we are trying to engage. Choosing a meaningful subject the writer can embrace is crucial to using this type of story to break down the walls that hinder discussions of composing, as this third and final ending illustrates.

"Well," I start. But I don't know what to say or how to continue, so this 'well' of mine hangs in mid-air for a while, floating between us while she continues to stare daggers. Suddenly, I remember a conversation that I caught the tail end of as Nancy left her friend to enter the writing center.

"Do you watch *The X-Files*?"

"Yeah. Why?" She draws out her answer, as if thinking she is about to commit to some unspeakable task.

"I was just thinking about last week's episode about the writer." I stop for a breath—and a reaction, which I promptly get.

"What about it?" She's not making it easier, but I'm ready.

"Well, I thought it was really interesting how he would follow Scully around, think about her motives, go home, and write . . ."

". . . more chapters about her." She completes my sentence as I nod in agreement.

"Why do you think he needs to keep watching her?"

"Because he wanted to see if he really understands her, I guess."

"Why?" I hope to push just a little further, and I hold my breath while I wait for her answer.

"Well, because he might need to add something to get her character, you know, right. On target."

I take the plunge. "What if we just looked at your paper here and thought about what other things we might add that would make your paper on target? We don't have to cut anything right now. We could just see what adding and shuffling might do for another version, à la 'X-Files' style."

Nancy's crisp nod—ever so brief—encourages me. I turn back to the paper with renewed vigor.

Complicating Matters

Ambiguous and difficult to define, stories do have the power to break down barriers between tutors and writers. Some writers feel alienated from their writing and by their image of the tutor, who may appear to them as an apparition of a teacher. Stories are a way of building a relationship and finding that difficult balance between the academic and the personal meanings that college life demands. Stories can help writers see through the experiences of other writers—you, Hemingway, even a shadowy writer from *The X-Files*—that the struggle to communicate ideas isn't a solitary battle. Some final thoughts:

Stories are not the answer for every barrier between tutors and writers. Despite the advantages of stories, they don't always work. Writers will not follow the path you want them to; stories don't always create a happy ending in which you feel wonderful and the writer leaves inspired to write thirty more pages. Think about what you want your stories to achieve, and gauge reactions. What kind of response are you getting? What additional techniques are you going to use in addition to stories? We all think differently, so use stories that you have planned out ahead of time. If your story falls flat, go to Plan B and try to make your point another way.

Stories may reveal personal information. We can talk about our own experiences, but we need to keep in mind that in doing so, we reveal a part of ourselves. We are giving someone else a glimpse of who we are. In other words, share carefully. You're at work, not a social activity, so choose stories that are appropriate for both the writer you are talking with and the educational environment you are in. (See Agostinelli, Poch, and Santoro, this volume.)

Stories have quantity limits, so know when to say when. Telling story after story may not be the best way to conduct a tutoring session. A successful tutor has many different strategies to choose from, storytelling being only one. Your goal is to help writers begin a dialogue about their writing and revising process. Don't waste time rambling, or they may be confused or angry with you when they leave. What is one important story you can use?

Stories are a two-way street: listening is as important as telling. If the stories we tell are important, the stories that students tell are equally important. Listen to all of the conversation, not just the "writing" parts. What insight do students reveal that helps you understand them? What do they say that helps you understand why they might have erected barriers between themselves and you?

If our goal is to help students feel comfortable with us so that we can talk about their writing, we need to make sure that we reach out with words that create safe spaces for them to enter the conversation. Stories can help to create this space.

Further Reading

Murray, Donald M. 1996. *Crafting a Life in Essay, Story, and Poem*. Portsmouth, NH: Heinemann Boynton/Cook.

In this work, Murray goes beyond the basic techniques of composing essays, stories, and poems to discuss the mental and emotional attitudes that, combined with skills, encourage writing. Tutors will appreciate Murray's clear and engaging writing style.

Murray, Donald M. 1982. *Learning by Teaching*. Portsmouth, NH: Heinemann Boynton/Cook.

Another informative and interesting Murray text for understanding the importance of not only talking but listening in conferences with writers. Murray blends stories of his own while talking about composing and interacting with students both person to person and writer to writer.

Trimmer, Joseph F., ed. 1997. *Narration as Knowledge: Tales of the Teaching Life*. Portsmouth, NH: Heinemann Boynton/Cook.

To learn more about storytelling in academic settings, this is a great place for tutors to start, with chapters covering a variety of topics and a great source list for further references on narrative theory.

Witherell, Carol, and Nel Nodding, eds. 1991. *Stories Lives Tell: Narrative and Dialogue in Education*. NY: Teachers College Press.

Arranged into three separate sections that tackle narratives, benefits for tellers and listeners, and educational implications, this book can help tutors understand how stories are a part of one's sense of self and how they help in constructing meaning.

Notes

1. Nancy Mason Bradbury, *Writing Aloud: Storytelling in Late Medieval England* (Urbana, IL: University of Illinois Press, 1998), 5.

2. Brian Fox Ellis, "Why Tell Stories?" *Storytelling Magazine,* January 1997, 21.

3. Richard J. Meyer, *Stories from the Heart: Teachers and Students Researching Their Literacy Lives* (Mahwah, NJ: Lawrence Erlbaum Associates, 1996), 4.

4. Betty D. Roe, Suellen Alfred, and Sandy Smith, *Teaching Through Stories: Yours, Mine, and Theirs* (Norwood, MA : Christopher Gordon Publishers, 1998), 4.

5. Christina Murphy and Steve Sherwood, eds., *The St. Martin's Sourcebook for Writing Tutors* (NY: St. Martin's Press, 1995), 1.

6. Pamela B. Farrell, ed., *The High School Writing Center: Establishing and Maintaining One* (Urbana, IL: National Council of Teachers of English, 1989), 145.

Works Cited

Bradbury, N. M. 1998. *Writing Aloud: Storytelling in Late Medieval England.* Urbana, IL: University of Illinois Press.

Ellis, B. F. 1997. "Why Tell Stories?" *Storytelling Magazine.* Jan.: 21–3.

Farrell, P. B., ed. 1989. *The High School Writing Center: Establishing and Maintaining One.* Urbana: NCTE.

Meyer, R. J. 1996. *Stories from the Heart: Teachers and Students Researching Their Literacy Lives.* Mahwah, NJ: Lawrence Erlbaum Associates.

Murphy, C., and S. Sherwood, eds. 1995. *The St. Martin's Sourcebook for Writing Tutors.* New York: St. Martin's Press.

Roe, B. D., S. Alfred, and S. Smith. 1998. *Teaching Through Stories: Yours, Mine, and Theirs.* Norwood, MA: Christopher Gordon Publishers.

6

Is There a Creative Writer in the House?

Tutoring to Enhance Creativity and Engagement

Wendy Bishop

Creative writing. Have you ever wondered what *un*creative writing would be and why anyone would aim for the same? Ditto *un*critical thinking. I believe that all engaged writers are both critical and creative. How could they aim not to be? So even as I offer ideas for looking at the tutoring session with creativity in mind, I don't think of my advice here as merely adding a technique, or spicing up the session, or putting icing on the tutorial cake. Instead, this perspective is meant to encourage you to help writers to think-like-a-writer-thinks (and I hope that's the perspective you take too).

Some Background

Peter Elbow believes that we need to like our writing to perform well at it. Donald Murray says that all writing is to some degree autobiographical. Both claims suggest writers need to be engaged with the text, no matter who assigns it, or for what purposes. Too often, the clients we see in writing centers are lacking a connection, a spark, a perspective. Not unreasonable, given the conditions of institutional schooling. Writers who come to work with us may view writing as not theirs, the role of writer as not theirs, and the joys of writing as forever out of their reach. Giving them some insight, providing them with some writers' rules-of-thumb and practical practices can often be just what it takes to guide them to greater engagement.

Greater engagement usually equals greater investment. And greater investment—even if it doesn't result in immediate, dramatic improvement in the

SEE DISCUSSION TOPIC **#3** AT THE END OF THIS BOOK

text at hand—generally has long-term effects. Positive engagement prompts the writer you work with to spend more time with a text. And more time with a text—with that one, this one, and the next one—is the only sure road to better writing. Creative writers know that. They are infamous for telling you how long and hard they work at their craft. "The problem of creative writing," says poet Steven Spender, "is essentially one of concentration, and the supposed eccentricities of poets are usually due to mechanical habits or rituals developed in order to concentrate."[1]

Lack of concentration, poor work habits, counterproductive rituals push writers away from their texts. So does discouragement. Studies of basic writers in the 1970s and 1980s proved how discouraging text work was for writers who were not supported, encouraged, or engaged. Researchers like Lillian Bridwell-Bowles, Sondra Perl, Nancy Sommers, Mike Rose, and others found that the basic writers they observed and talked to were stuck at the local level—worrying over spelling, worrying over the presentation of self, worrying over a crippling number of lower-level writing issues. They never had a chance to engage, soar, create, discover, learn about self and others, family and community, to think through writing.

Not only that, most student writers just don't make or take the time needed to make significant progress with their writing. And, of course, their lives are busy: "Adrianna provides a profile of work habits typical of other students in her class. She takes five classes, works twenty hours each week, and spends six to ten hours per week on homework," says Susan Wyche in a recent study.[2] Interviewing students like Adrianna, Wyche found that they didn't have the space or habits of concentration that Stephen Spender claims is so crucial to creative work, that we know is crucial to getting work done at all:

> Adrianna has difficulty creating and following through on self-made schedules. Her problems are further compounded by being unable to concentrate for extended periods of time; instead, she takes numerous breaks, including watching television. By her own account she begins drafts cold, using only the hour prior to drafting to give the paper serious thought.[3]

It's not surprising, actually, that tutorials alone can spark creativity in our students by providing them a place and sustained opportunity to think through writing—a place and an opportunity they find or make nowhere else in their busy lives. Writers are people who write. Just that.

No positive feedback? No reason to move forward. No bag of tools and tricks? No alternatives. No time? No place? No plan? Then no way to vault out of a corner, leap out of a pit, improvise, riff, discover, and uncover. Writers need flexible rules of thumb, heuristics, and a sense of when to use what, where, when, how, and why. They need writing center tutors to help them find their ways. So let's look at some.

What to Do

Getting Started

Where do writers' ideas come from? From reading in the broadest sense—
reading other writers, reading one's own life, reading the world around us. As
a student of poetry and later as a teacher of writing, I learned to read other writers backwards. Call this a sort of tongue-in-cheek version of the weighty literary giant deconstruction. "What," I'd speculate, "might have prompted this
poem about . . . love, death, life? What can I see going on technically at the
word, sentence, whole-text level that I could copy (steal?), celebrate by borrowing? What is going on thematically that resonates to my own life?"

Asking such questions, I'd work backwards from product to process. Famous examples? *Romeo and Juliet* becomes *West Side Story.* The laconic prose
style of Ernest Hemingway is everywhere imitated. But here's the secret: what
works as a technique for uncovering, deconstructing, understanding literary
genres holds true of the more technical and transactional genres of writing in
our lives. We don't re-invent the phone book each time one is assembled, we al-
phabetize. We respect a moving college application essay when we read it—
and we can analyze it rhetorically to see how the writer appealed to us, moved
and persuaded us to see her as the best possible candidate for our program. Web
'zine sites become popular because they "work," but we can look at any textual
"work" for its constituent parts—what language does it use, what voice, sentence style, organizing strategy, daring effects? And as tutors we need to help
writers come to these understandings—to argue and articulate how they read,
what they read, and why they read.

To encourage careful reading and imitation (I mean in the best sense—set
by the writer, not set as a lesson in writing-as-punishment),

- **Try What-ifs.** What if I recast my opening paragraph in short declarative
  Hemingway-esque or circular Gertrude Steinian sentences? Will I be able
  to harvest a passage of declarative or rhythmically circular prose?

To encourage idea generation if your writer (and you) are short of ideas,

- **Try Something-likes.** Which kind of writing that I admire is something
  like the writing I'm doing? Then, what of those something-like writings—
  theme or style or both—might I import into this text?

To explore options, to open up new avenues,

- **Try Lots-ofs.** Lots of X writing goes like this. Therefore, I could do some
  X and then add some Y writing to vary, complicate, and add interest to my
  X writing.

And finally,

- **Collect start-up exercises.** Here's where creative writing textbooks can offer you specific, stealable advice, tricks, tools, tries. Realize that an inven-

tion prompt for a poem can often add spice to an essay. Michael Walters, for instance, suggests: "Write a line of poetry that seems to be an opening line . . . then be prepared to give your line away. . . . [after discussion of the lines] the author of the line agrees to give it—no strings attached and forever—to the student whose suggestion, enthusiasm, or oddball approach most pleases him/her."[4] I think you can see how this can work in a composition classroom. But it can also work in a one to one or small group tutorial where first lines are brainstormed together, discussed, and then "auctioned off," that is, chosen to allow the writer a first start or a solid new start.

Realize that most writers mix and match genres. That inventions work in clusters—writing about memory, food, family, often take us to the same early childhood wells of inspiration. Robin Behn and Chase Twichell have put together a useful book for poets in *The Practice of Poetry.* Natalie Goldberg in her two popular books, *Wild Mind* and *Writing Down the Bones,* offers Zen-inspired prompts and advice. (See Further Reading.) Elaine Farris in *Writing from the Inner Self* begins with the writer and moves outward, including excellent prompts for descriptively emphasizing the five senses. My own book, *Released into Language,* offers two chapters of multigenre prompts, including writing intentionally cliched works to learn the perils and uses of cliches. A second book, *Elements of Alternate Style,* encourages stylistic experimentations. And an early tutor training book, *Training Tutors for Writing Center Conferences* by Thomas Reigstad and Donald McAndrew, offers a series of tutorial-based prompts—a composing exercise to get even the most topic-free writer into a topic of personal interest, to development techniques like nutshelling (similar to paraphrasing). (See Trupe, this volume.)

For creative critical responses, there's no finer resource than Peter Elbow and Pat Belanoff's *Sharing and Responding.* One of my favorite of their response techniques asks a reader to describe "What's Almost Said or Implied." What do you think the writer is going to say but doesn't? What ideas seem to hover around the edges? What do you end up wanting to hear more about?[5] I take this exercise one step further by encouraging the writer to name what prompts them to feel this way about their own texts—are there textual, tonal, or syntactic clues? Can this missing-ness be heard in the writer's voice as she reads aloud to you? The why of it all is what your writer needs to learn—to see with you, to see for himself.

From my use of that book and my collaboration with other creative writing teachers like Hans Ostrom and Katharine Haake, I've developed some "continuing on techniques" that I encourage writers and their tutors to try.

Continuing On by Revising Out

Sometimes a writer has an idea. But not enough text. The writer you're working with has a desire to be engaged, but hasn't gotten rolling so isn't really. Engaged, that is. I ask flat out for what I call a "fat draft." Next draft is doubled.

One paragraph must become two, two pages four, and so on. No questions asked, no judgments made. At this point, not (necessarily) better but more.

For the writer who already has a mass of text but isn't ready to revise down (where we cut off rather than open possibilities), I ask for a shadow draft and/or post-outlining. For a shadow draft, the writer reads over his text once, then turns the paper over and returns to the computer or the paper and pen, and begins again. What was most important remains salient and reappears, what was not important has fallen aside. The new draft may be the best draft or the best new draft may be a recombination—a word milkshake—taken from the two. Writers know that sometimes many, many more than two drafts make up the real textual volume of a final text, but shadow drafts somehow sound less threatening. More on shadow drafting can be found in a forthcoming textbook, *Metro,* by Ostrom, Bishop, and Haake.

Postoutlining   No, outlining isn't all bad. Done to force thought and the writer and the text into a pre-ordained mold, it can constrain and constrict. But outlining can also be a creative tool when used at the right time. Ask the writer to read the text paragraph by paragraph. After each paragraph has been shared, together find the center-of-gravity sentence—the central idea or thesis. If not a single solid sentence, then summarize the gist of the passage in one sentence. Write it down. Go on, find the next one in the next paragraph, and the next. Then look at what's there. Not a B for every A or a II for every I. But a rough skeleton of thought in motion. Now, think about reorganization as potential and possibility. What ghostly, missing paragraphs still could be or need to be written? Why?

Consider together what would happen to this text if the writer changed or mixed genres. We know this happens anyway—the effective argumentative paper often begins with a dramatic narrative lead. Sometimes there may be room for a diary entry, a poem, an aphorism, a quote, in a seemingly straight-arrow, down-the-right-hand-margin, traditional paper. What would, how could you and the writer argue for this? (Hint—most down-the-margin student work is a devalued genre we could label schoolwriting.) What do you and this writer need to do to make yourselves and other in-the-world-writers actually want to get involved with this text? Would you really read on if you didn't have to? If not, take a risk and make this text—at least for one draft—a text you would choose to read.

Predict the future   Finally, where else could this piece go? Characterize its form. Use a metaphor—it looks like a pear, it's got the zig-zagging organization of an English garden maze or a computer game. Is that what seems best for the writer, the occasion, the reader? Decide together on how to capitalize on the strengths of this draft. Talk about this. What is done well and could be done more? Writers need space and excess—lots of words, lots of pages, lots of experiments. Without experimentation, and some falling back for recalibration (let's call it this instead of failure), foreword movement can't take place.

Continuing On by Revising In

Okay. Urban sprawl. We know it. Daily, we enter many arenas of textual sprawl. The windy legal brief. The belabored letter to the editor. The paper where everyone offered good advice and the eager writer—your client, perhaps—added, and added, and added, and now has too many leads, too many paths to take or abandon, too much. Still, this is good. Think of the metaphors at hand: pruning, shaping, selecting, highlighting, dramatizing. (Let's consider these, although even as I put down one metaphor two others grow in its place.)

Prune   Think of this as global and/or local removal of deadweight. Globally. Through postoutlining (yes, maybe a second time), a writer can learn to see repeats. Most of my essays begin three or four times and I find this true of the work I help edit too. Look for the place where you both want to slap down an arrow and say, "This text starts here." Should the writer trim? reshuffle? reorganize? At the local level, pruning suggests some words need to disappear. After doing sentences, do the same for words: change two to one—the right one, the precise one, the effective one. Tune and tauten. Look for clunky first-breath clauses and sentences and enjoy trying them six different ways, together. You each write three. You both vote. One stays. The writer has pruned the original down and tossed other attempts. It's worth it. You find confusing words and play dictionary and thesaurus together—what do you think this word means? What does it generally mean? How is it meaning here, and is it meaning what the writer thinks it means and needs it to mean?

Shaping and Selecting   What textual space does the writer really have? Has he written 2000 words in pursuit of a solid 500-word response? That's fine. Shape and select. Does he want something circular? This is good in a long piece where he may need to remind us of the beginning when we reach the ending. But in a small 500-word space, maybe the economical traditional is most effective—a killer first sentence, then support, and a zinger ending. Maybe though, your writer finds a new rhythm by shaking out one sentence into the next. Link sentences by words (repeat key words), or images (extend a metaphor). Now's the time to look at how she uses all her tools (words, syntax, register, and so on) to weave the text together in order to tie down a reader's attention.

Before revising in, perhaps the writer rigorously revised out, writing too many comparisons and analogies and taking too many side trips. Ask the writer to survey the landscape, to catalog the ones she has and select: Which is most useful for her purposes? Which seems newest? Like any seasoning, try to figure out how much is too much, how much is just right. Read aloud. Listen to the shape and selection. You both can hear what is going on. Then articulate it so it can go on again in the next text, helping your writer to concentrate by internalizing these skills.

Highlighting and Dramatizing   We live in the brave new world of Webs. Don't forget that mixing genres helps add interest and that the tools and techniques of the technical writer and Web composer are out there for the borrowing—in small doses. As in dress and hair color, we need to match effect to occasion. But here's where your writer starts thinking more of audience/reader.

◆   For instance, wouldn't a bullet list let each question stand out, helping my future reader find her way?

Midway through drafting this chapter I knew I would come back and try to help you out with new formatting. It's fun to run on draft ideas. But I owe it to you to help you through the thicket. So I can bullet or diamond list. I can italicize and clip art and hypertext. But remember, this is all coming after the fact. If my process has worked, I've said something and now I want to make you feel it like I feel it. I don't want my drama to stand in for substance (it won't, never fooled anyone that way), but I do like using it to help you find your readerly way and hear my writerly voice. There. Here. The same holds true for you and the writer in a tutorial.

Editing and Proofing

The two tricks I use most often in writing classes actually come from lessons I've learned in tutorial sessions and the desire to make writing more actively engaging.

Wall editing   I ask all writers in a class to stand (must not sit—leads to sleepiness) and read the text aloud and make first corrections. Tutors and tutees have long read to and for each other. But try this. Foolishness wakes us up. Have your writer stand and read aloud to the wall and you can quietly take notes of things you might mention later. Before you do mention them, the writer will have heard/seen/found several spots to talk about.

Swap editing   Edit someone else, but only off-text (only the author marks on the text). In group tutorials, this can lead to small group discussions. Why did this writer place a comma after all conjunctions (and, or, so, for, but, yet) and this writer didn't? Just what is the convention anyway?

About this time, I imagine you are saying, What's so creative about this? This is tutoring? My response: Exactly!

Georgia Heard writes, "At a recent workshop I asked people to list where poems hide in their lives. Here are some of the places they named: in my father's chair, in spider webs attached to the walls of the garage, in the taste of spinach in my mouth, in my mother's silence."[6] And here I'll borrow again. Where do the texts your students bring to you in writing centers really come from? Where do they hide in their lives? Ask this of them actively, and those texts will arrive and begin to grow.

I think active tutoring, collaborative discussions of writing progress, concentrated periods for attention to texts, creates space for creativity and engagement in writing. Writer and reader are always co-creating meaning in a text. From my point of view, it's essential that tutors be practicing writers—that means sometimes basic writers and sometimes wildly successful writers—but most often living somewhere in between. (Note: I can make anyone a basic writer. Here's your assignment: In five minutes, write a Shakespearean sonnet.) The more you try out these techniques, the more you'll be able to help the client you work with tailor them to the current tutoring situation. That means, too, collecting a few books on writing, like those listed in this chapter and throughout this collection.

That also means, read rhetorically and read for style, all the time, whenever you can. By analyzing the styles of writing you encounter in the world you'll become a more proficient brainstormer and adviser to your clients on the options available to them. Let's face it. We don't look the same, dress the same. Why should our prose? Then, put all these bits of advice in service of helping the writers you work with interrogate convention and experimentation as tandem parts of the writing process. Without one, there's not the other. Without the convention of workplace dress codes, dress down Friday means nothing. Without mystery and romance writing, literary genres have no backdrop and no way to achieve a false sense of superiority. And vice versa. Without carefully constructing the lab report, plunging into research writing, or digging in and taking a strong position, the college student is only partially educated in the conventions of the academy, no matter how many impressionistic and self-satisfying poems he writes late at night in the dorm. Not either/or but both/and.

Complicating Matters

Well, I can raise some arguments for you. Since I'm just finishing drafting, you can't possibly raise them for yourselves.

You: I'm faced with a student who wants a paper fixed and doesn't care about drafting out and drafting in. They want to draft done.

Me: That's why I acknowledged that some of these tries won't result in a better immediate text. This is a matter of philosophy—mine, yours, that of the center you work in. For me, it's important to help the student to experience writing as a writer and to get further along on the path of lifelong literacy. I understand there are many other philosophies and many other daily forces at work on the tutoring scene, but this is always my tacit if not my explicit stance. I don't mind being dual: tutoring for the conventions and tutoring unconventionally, because I think this is how we learn best, as writers.

You: I don't like to write all that much, as much as you're suggesting. I'm a good editor and that's proved to be what most of my clients want to hear about from me.

Me: Maybe I'm a little evangelical here but I do believe writing is one of the best ways to improve any lot in life—to learn how to think more deeply, to understand the self better, to work out problems, to clarify beliefs, and to evaluate experiences. I'd ask you to do both/and here. Don't give up your pride in your editing and don't fail to please your clients with those skills but do notice how you may be improving as a writer through the act of tutoring and writing with your client and how those skills are equally to be valued. Then write some more. (There, I can't help but be evangelical.)

You: Tutorials go by too fast for these activities. You don't understand my writing center situation . . .

Me: I do realize all my suggestions have to be adapted to local contexts. But also I do write from an understanding of contemporary theory and research into writing and reading that suggests there are commonalities of process and purpose that undergird all acts of composing. I've tried to draw from that research, to make suggestions that can be tailored to tutorial, client, and center in ways that are helpful. You are the expert here—start from what you know. But just as a writer must start into new territory at many points in a drafting process, consider what you can learn from some of these new (if they are new to you) techniques and attitudes toward tutoring.

My sense is this—if you look to the invention-based exercises found in some of the books listed next, you'll discover writing prompts that engage you. You'll try them and you'll like the results of some of those tries. You'll enter the next tutorial, with an experience-based enthusiasm that lets you recommend similar activities to your clients. You'll both be engaged. You'll both be creative. You'll both be learning about writing—at the same time—for the day's text, for texts in the future. Writers write. Positive writing experiences make more writing. There's a math metaphor around here waiting to be thrown in—something about compound interest and exponential growth when you have a writer in the house, when you and your client are both writers in the writing center. But I'm going to throw in the towel instead, and let you take that last step yourself.

Further Reading

Behn, Robin, and Chase Twichell, eds. 1992. *The Practice of Poetry: Writing Exercises from Poets Who Teach.* New York: HarperPerennial.

Practicing poets suggest guided inventions: starting poems; focusing on image and metaphor; exploring self and subject; shaping inventions into forms; exploring sound and line; and experimenting with revision. Tutors will enjoy reading the sample poems and suggestions for further reading.

Bernays, Anne, and Pamela Painter. 1995. *What If? Writing Exercises for Fiction Writers.* New York: HarperCollins.

Here is a sourcebook of invention exercises such as "journey of the long sentence" and "practice writing good, clean prose"; the text encourages writers to become more involved with their drafts and includes samples of completed exercises by students.

Elbow, Peter, and Pat Belanoff. 1995. *Sharing and Responding.* 2nd ed. New York: McGraw-Hill.

What to say about a piece of writing? The authors offer alternative response methods for readers, writers, conferencing, workgroups and workshops, as well as suggestions for helping writers share work and perform descriptive, analytic, reader-based, and criterion-based responses.

Goldberg, Natalie. 1990. *Wild Mind: Living the Writer's Life.* New York: Bantam.

This book offers sixty-two, writer-, workgroup-, and workshop-related narrative discussions, most with a suggested exercise; it includes general writing topics and focuses on helping writers to improve their writing habits.

Notes

1. Brewster Ghiselin, *The Creative Process* (NY: Mentor/Penguin, 1952), 113.

2. Susan Wyche, "Time, Tools, Talismans," in *The Subject Is Writing: Essays by Teachers and Students,* 2nd ed., ed. Wendy Bishop (Portsmouth, NH: Heinemann Boynton/Cook, 1999), 32.

3. Wyche, 33.

4. Michael Walters, "Auction: First Lines," in *The Practice of Poetry: Writing Exercises from Poets Who Teach,* eds. Robin Behn and Chase Twichell (NY: HarperPerennial, 1992), 15.

5. Peter Elbow and Pat Belanoff, *Sharing and Responding.* 2nd ed. (NY: McGraw-Hill, 1995), 16.

6. Georgia Heard, *Writing Toward Home* (Portsmouth, NH: Heinemann, 1995), 11.

Works Cited

Bishop, W., ed. 1997. *Elements of Alternate Style: Essays on Writing and Revision.* Portsmouth, NH: Heinemann Boynton/Cook.

———. 1998. *Released into Language: Options for Teaching Creative Writing.* 2nd ed. Portsmouth, ME: Calendar Islands.

Elbow, P. 1993. "Ranking, Evaluating, and Liking: Sorting Out Three Forms of Judgment." *College English* 55: 187–206.

Farris, E. 1992. *Writing from the Inner Self.* NY: HarperPerennial.

Ghiselin, B. 1952. *The Creative Process.* NY: Mentor/Penguin.

Goldberg, N. 1986. *Writing Down the Bones: Freeing the Writer Within.* Boston: Shambhala.

Heard, G. 1995. *Writing Toward Home.* Portsmouth, NH: Heinemann.

Hughes, E. F. 1991. *Writing from the Inner Self.* New York: HarperPerennial.

Reigstad, T. J., and D. McAndrew. 1984. *Training Tutors for Writing Center Conferences.* Urbana, IL: National Council of Teachers of English.

Murray, D. 1991. "All Writing Is Autobiography." *College Composition and Communication* 42: 66–74.

Ostrom, H., W. Bishop, and K. Haake. Forthcoming. *Metro: A Guide to Writing Creatively.* New York: Longman.

Walters, M. 1992. "Auction: First Lines." In *The Practice of Poetry: Writing Exercises from Poets Who Teach,* eds. R. Behn and C. Twichell, 15–16. NY: HarperPerennial.

Wyche, S. 1999. "Time, Tools, Talismans." In *The Subject Is Writing: Essays by Teachers and Students,* 2nd ed., ed. W. Bishop, 30–42. Portsmouth, NH: Heinemann Boynton/Cook.

7

Style in the Writing Center

It's a Matter of Choice and Voice

Lea Masiello

What is style and how do you talk about it with writers? Talking about style may at first sound tedious, difficult, and highly regulated by handbook rules, and you may feel an instinct to avoid it altogether in writing center tutorials. But don't back off from a session on style; approach it instead with relish and enthusiasm because a contemporary approach to talking about style lets you focus on the writer's voice. To talk about voice, focus on the choices writers make that give the reader a sense of the person behind the words. In this chapter, I offer tutors some ideas about how to help writers so that they can link their stylistic choices to voice, purpose, subject, and audience.

When writers ask for help with their style, tutors don't have to get snarled in lengthy discussions about structural features. Conversations about style have always been part of the discussion of writing, yet the way in which we talk about style has changed over the years. We no longer use the eighteenth-century approach that focused on ornamentation or embellishment, approaches that treated style as decoration. Nor are we primarily concerned with practicing high or low styles, an approach that emphasized language as belonging to particular social and economic classes. Instead, we're more interested in whether written style is appropriate and effective in a specific context and for a clear purpose. A definition of voice that is helpful in talking about style comes recently from Donna Hickey, who, in her book *Developing a Written Voice,* explains that voice is "the writer's relationship to subject, audience, and occasion, as it is revealed through the particular speech patterns you hear as you read." [1] You can use this definition to begin a conversation about style.

SEE DISCUSSION TOPIC **#3** AT THE END OF THIS BOOK

Tutor: What is this essay about?

Writer: We had to write about a decision we made and its consequences so I wrote about my decision to get a butterfly tattoo and how people around me reacted.

Tutor: Would you read this aloud to me, please? I'll listen for places where I really hear your voice coming through loud and strong. I'll point those out to you and we'll talk about the choices you made that led to an effective voice. Then you can decide whether or not to make more choices like that to improve your style.

Hickey also describes voice as the "sum effect of all the stylistic choices a writer makes to communicate" to a particular audience.[2] A tutor's job in a session about style is to help the writer describe the effect he or she wants to create and then to help the writer make the stylistic choices needed to make this effect pervasive. If the tutor understands the strong relationship between voice and style, then the tutor has the means to talk about the specific elements that, combined, constitute style: word choice, sentence variation, rhythmic patterns, and emphasis. When you begin a conversation about voice and style, you will want to consider the writer's audience for the essay. Most likely, students are writing for their instructor, but they might also be writing for their classmates—for a class publication, for example. They might also be writing a letter to an editor for a local or school newspaper. These audiences are very specific and involve well-known relationships that help a writer think about how they want to sound to that reader.

Tutor: Let's talk a little about the audience for your essay about your tattoo. Do you know who will be reading this other than your instructor?

Writer: I know that we're going to exchange drafts in small groups for peer review, and we'll be putting together a class magazine at the end of the semester, so I guess I need to write for both the instructor and my classmates.

Tutor: That can be tricky. How do you want to sound for these two audiences?

Writer: I think I can sound informal for both audiences, you know, just like myself, although I'll want to not use any slang because the instructor will be grading it. Because my classmates are reading it, I want to be sure it's really interesting, maybe a little funny, but full of feeling.

Tutor: I know that I always got great feedback from my professors when I wrote in my natural voice, and when I brought in some humor, they loved it! Has your instructor made any comments in class about the kind of voice you should project?

Writer: He only told us to be ourselves.

Getting from the professor's comments on the essay to a discussion about voice might take a little finesse because of the way in which the written comments' voice, which is considered very close to our personality and opinions, may make a writer feel—defensive, insulted, offended. When a writer comes to a tutor for help with style and has comments like "awkward, rewrite more clearly" on her essay, you might expect the writer to be discouraged. That little jack of all trades, "awk," is especially problematic and frustrating to work with. How can any reader imagine what another reader found "awkward" and unclear without specific descriptions of how meaning broke down? You can puzzle about what the professor might want the writer to work on, or you can proceed to a new consideration of how the writer meant to sound and what choices she made consciously or unintentionally to create her voice. After a brief review of the instructor's response and an explanation of how style connects to audience and voice, forge ahead with a new consideration and leave the bad feelings behind.

Because I wanted to find out how other writing teachers approach discussions of style, I asked sixteen of my colleagues at IUP and other schools to tell me how they define style, how they teach style to their students, and what they would like to see tutors talk about during tutorial sessions focused on style. There was a pleasing consensus that the tutorial conversation should be about voice. And passion! And most of all, choice. Many instructors noted that they spend numerous class sessions playing around with audience, experimenting with changing voices appropriately for different kinds of readers so that students can see how we make choices that depend on what we think our audience expects from us. Looking at the elements of voice, passion, and choice in terms of style will help us identify some very workable strategies for a tutorial session. I hope that you'll see that tutorials on style can be an opportunity for delight—and even menace—with words instead of a tedious exercise in detangling grammar.

Some Background

If we say that choice 'n' voice define style we have a starting point for discussing research about style. There have been significant changes in our approaches to style, although some basic principles endure: syntactic variety, figurative language, and character have always been part of the discussion about style. Early classical rhetoricians such as Plato and Aristotle believed that style can be discussed in terms of ethos or character, a presentation of self that helps a speaker become a persuasive and convincing orator. You might be surprised at the attention these philosophers gave to the way in which speakers and writers conveyed their moral character through their language choices. They were very concerned that speakers and writers understand how powerful and influential language can be in affecting the ideas of others, and wanted to be sure that the links between language choice, values, and moral character be clearly represented. To understand the relevance of this principle today, take a look at advertising for cigarettes and notice how the language is chosen to persuade the reader that smoking is beneficial to you—it can make you more beautiful, more attractive, cooler in every way—when, in fact, we know that it is bad for you in every way.

Another difference in the way that we talk about style today as opposed to historical approaches is that we no longer emphasize style as ornamentation. That is, it is not usually part of your development as a contemporary college writer to learn how to manipulate various tropes and figures in order to impress your reader. However, learning how to use different kinds of figurative language can help writers develop a stylistic repertoire, and you will see that figurative language is still covered in contemporary rhetorics and handbooks. Figurative language can be a powerful way to develop voice and character and to build a bridge between the writer and reader. Metaphor builds upon common experiences but makes readers work a little harder to make connections between their own experiences and the writer's new ideas and experiences. The effort that readers put into unpacking a metaphor brings them closer to the writer and helps them engage with interesting and novel ideas.

Tutor: Writing about yourself as an emerging butterfly seems really important to you, right?

Writer: Oh yes. I want my reader to understand how I'm feeling about growing and changing in college, as a student and a woman. It's a struggle to get out of the cocoon, but the challenge is worth it because of how beautiful the result will be.

Metaphor can be a way of tapping into the writer's personal expression, values, and feelings. Relating character and metaphor can lead to productive conversations about voice and thus style. For example, consider this conversation about choosing a voice for the essay that one of my students wrote recently on getting a tattoo:

Tutor: What kind of person do you want your reader to imagine is behind this essay about getting a tattoo?

Writer: The reader might think that because I have a tattoo I'm really weird or wild or something, but I want to stress how I was very careful. It's also important to me that I chose a butterfly picture for my tattoo to show how I'm changing into a beautiful young woman, so I want to sound sort of elegant.

Tutor: How will you do that? What kinds of words do you want to use?

Writer: I could use some words that sound beautiful and elegant. But I also want to just be myself, use my normal language, I think. If I explain how I went about choosing a tattoo artist and thought ahead of time about the results, that should show how serious I was.

Recently, scholars commenting on style encourage other teachers to have their students take risks with style, consciously break rules (and have a good reason for doing so), and be playful and imaginative. This approach puts a new burden on the tutor: you have to know how to break rules effectively and you have to be prepared to have fun! Scholars believe that this alternative approach to style is a way of bringing freedom into the art of writing, and the collaboration between tutor and writer in this liberating approach puts the tutor at the vanguard of building a new discourse community that values choice and risk above sticking to the rules. Some specific ideas about this playful approach to style come from a collection of essays edited by Wendy Bishop, *Elements of Alternate Style,* inspired by Winston Weathers (see Bishop this volume). Writing in 1970, Weathers emphasized that through style, we prove our individuality and express our values and attitudes, and most importantly, we demonstrate our freedom.[3] As you help others become more varied, flexible language users, you help them become people who will have more control and influence in their words. In an e-mail interview in *Elements of Alternate Style,* Winston Weathers defines a good writer as someone who should "know how to design and build all kinds of structures," so that writers have a variety of techniques available.[4] By working next to the writer as she crafts and recrafts, you are establishing with her the language community that her stylistic choices fit into. You help her see how expression, choice, and word power give her a stronger role and identity in daily activities.

At the same time, tutors should keep another position in mind that Elizabeth Rankin discusses in her article "Revitalizing Style." The tutorial conference should be balanced, and draw upon both skillbuilding and the search for personal expression. Rankin reminds us that as much as we yearn to see writers grow personally and feel empowered, we must remember not to romanticize the search for voice, and to keep it grounded in the reality of words and choices.[5]

What to Do

Let's pick up the conversation about the essay on getting a tattoo as the tutor and writer venture into creative territory.

Tutor: How do you think you could liven this piece up while still achieving your goals? What kinds of changes could you make in your language that would be really creative here?

Writer: I'd like to describe some of the photos I saw in the tattoo artist's portfolio of his work. Some of them were really wild.

Tutor: Is there anything else you could add that might be a little unexpected, say, about what was running through your mind as you were getting the tattoo?

Writer: Yeah, well, I was imagining what my mother was going to say to me when she saw it!

Tutor: What else?

Writer: I was thinking about what my friends would think, and I was worrying about the pain I'd have later when it was healing.

Tutor: You could write what we call an 'interior monologue' to reveal your thoughts during the tattoo procedure.

Writer: I could write the conversation I had with my mother when she saw the tattoo. Could I quote her using some pretty rough language?

Tutor: I think so, as long as you make it clear that you're quoting her words. Getting a tattoo is a pretty risky thing, so you want to show what you were thinking about as you took that risk and then what really happened afterwards.

It isn't unusual today for young people to get tattoos, and although people with tattoos aren't stereotyped the way they used to be, it still represents a personal stylistic statement. When a person shows off a design sparkling on a shoulder or ankle, he might be revealing his character, attitude, or values. Just as many people today feel comfortable taking personal risks with their appearance, most professors are comfortable encouraging their students to take risks as writers. My conversations with colleagues about style and my review of current research have convinced me that we will see more research about the relationship among risk, voice, style, identity, and community. To learn more about style, voice, and identity, conduct your own research project. Ask other tutors in your writing center the following questions: How would you describe your style? What experiences led you to develop your style? How do you think we should help writers develop their styles?

More Strategies for Talking about Style: Focus on Choice

College students are in the process of deciding what kind of person they want to be and how they want others to see them. They worry about how they sound in their writing just as they worry about how they look. They may feel afraid to take on any new voices or personalities in their academic writing because they fear making choices that will lead to failure. They may have developed voices that have worked in high school, and they will want to hold onto them like their favorite worn and torn jeans. It pays to remind writers that in college they're expected to try out new ideas and styles. Varying stylistic choices in writing is a lot like choosing to put a butterfly tattoo on your shoulder, pierce your belly-button, or dye your hair pink: you don't know how it's going to look or feel until you try it, nor will you know what kind of response it will get from your friends and family until you do.

Trying out a new voice presumes that the writer knows how she sounds to begin with. That may not be the case. College writers may not know what kind of language they have been using in their essays, so you will want to help them describe how they have been sounding and then work toward reshaping a voice that they decide is appropriate for the assignment. To help bring out the voice and style most appropriate for their writing, ask the writer to tell you what he was trying to express. When you talk with a writer, help him get back to how he wanted to sound as he wrote. We are more likely to write awkwardly when instruction about how we're supposed to sound interferes with our intuition about how we want to sound. Both you and the writer will enjoy talking about how to break rules effectively, and most teachers will be delighted to read essays that show this amount of control and choice.

Not every professor wants students to develop their style by breaking rules, however, and you will work with many students who have been asked to conform to standard conventions of academic writing. Such conventions are easily found in grammar reference texts (and now on-line) and these books provide descriptive information about sentence structure and diction in units called style (see Eckard and Staben, this volume). You may be able to use such terms as "liveliness and appropriateness" or "variety and repetition" when working with a more advanced writer who has a grasp of grammatical approaches to revising.[6] A few instructors I know have used Joseph Williams' *Style: Ten Lessons in Clarity and Grace,* and although they find this book useful, they all warn that it's not for everyone because it presumes that you have a firm grasp of grammatical concepts.

Tap into Figurative Thought: Use Metaphors to Find a Voice

Another effective approach for helping writers develop their style is finding a metaphor to make stylistic choices. A few years ago a student in my writing class wrote a wonderful essay about learning to make go-carts with his uncle. His enthusiasm for constructing the carts and for learning from his uncle was brought out delightfully in the essay, and I felt the writer's pleasure and satisfaction. The only problem was that the sentences rolled into each other, like brakeless go-carts rolling down hills and smashing into trees. I read the essay aloud in class, much to everyone's pleasure, especially the writer's, who had always felt he was failure as a writer, and we all laughed and admired his work. Later, Matt and I talked about his voice, and I told him what a wonderful rollicking voice he had, but I added that he needed to get some control over it, just as he had learned how to get control over the brakes on the go-cart. The comparison worked; we didn't need to talk about grammar or to labor over comma splices and fragments. He just listened to his own voice a little differently, and then rewrote to put some brakes into his style. Matt's success illustrated the power of linking voice, style, and purpose through an umbrella-like metaphor, in this case, the voice of the go-carts with and without brakes, and a reckless and competent driver.

Another instructor in my survey described a visual strategy for controlling voice. The visual picture of voice that this technique creates provides a concrete way for the writer to confront their choices and decide what revisions are really best. Linda McPherson asks her composition students to "draw the face behind the writing" and then evaluate the face that emerges. Writers can decide if that's really the face they want or how to present a different face and then draw a new one. You can then ask the writer, "What changes can you make to create the face you want your reader to 'see'?"

Metaphors also help readers visualize the writer's passion and purpose. Nicole (not her real name) wanted a strong final statement about the importance of her tattoo, but she didn't know how to repeat her main idea without sounding maudlin. Her tutor suggested that she expand the comparison of her own growth to that of the metamorphosis of a butterfly.

Writer: I want to conclude by giving the reader a final picture of how the butterfly *is* me.

Tutor: Tell me again what the connection is between the butterfly and your identity?

Writer: I'm like a butterfly because I'm changing all the time. Not everybody feels good about change, but I thrive on it. Some people want to hold on to their old high school selves, but I'm ready to unfold my new wings and fly away.

Tutor: That's really a nice comparison. Describe specifically how a butterfly opens its wings gradually, maybe struggling a little at first, but then suddenly takes off in flight.

Use Models to Illustrate Voice and Choice

A number of teachers I surveyed described ways they use published writing to help students get ideas about voice and style. I would never advocate slavish imitation of a published writer's style, but I have seen students get excited about particular writers, their voices and ideas, and want to learn to "sound like him." Sometimes this happens unconsciously; after we've been reading an author, we might find ourselves picking up the rhythms, sounds, and structures without planning to do so. However, we can consciously experiment with imitation in order to practice writing that seems appealing to our own ears.

To find models for style, work with the books that students bring with them to the writing center. Anthologies commonly used in writing courses offer many different kinds of voices and style; ask the writer to identify an essay that he or she really liked and would enjoy sounding like. Then, ask the student to choose a paragraph and a set of two or three sentences to examine closely. It's important to look at sentences in a context of larger discourse such as a paragraph because writers make choices about style based on rhythms of sentences as they work together, not in isolation. With your tutee, look at the way in which the writer has varied structure and diction, length, and sound.

Top Five Tips for Tutoring Stylishly

Tutors want their tutees to leave a session with a revision plan and with some satisfaction that what they've discussed will lead to changes that will please the writer's professor. One worry tutors have is that they'll tell writers something that professors won't like. Writers must understand that they alone are responsible for making stylistic choices, and tutors must refrain from rewriting those "awkward" sentences. You'll need strategies to help writers come up with their own new words. Here are some concrete suggestions faculty shared with me:

1. Work with the writer's own voice to replace cliches with fresh expressions and new metaphors that come out of the writer's own experiences.

2. Demonstrate sentence-combining techniques to vary structure and emphasis.[7]

3. Break a rule when it serves your purpose.

4. Find your passion. Ask the writer, "What did you want me to feel when I read this?"

5. Write sentences so that the ending stresses an idea.

Complicating Matters: When Voice Is Not Supposed to Be Strong or Personal

Throughout this essay, I've chosen to focus on the relationship among voice, choice, and personal style. But what if you meet writers who aren't interested in having a personal style? Or writers who have been told to "keep yourself out of the prose," or "don't use I, contractions, dashes or parentheses." When your basic approach to tutoring stylishly fails because the writer cannot or doesn't want to put himself out there, then you have to emphasize developing style more by meeting the audience than by using a strong voice.

If you've thought, "I have to help the student in the way she wants and needs," you're on target in addressing audience. When students have been given strict guidelines for voice and style, it won't do anyone any good to fight this approach to writing. You can emphasize how the student is still making choices even when conforming to the prescriptions of the assignment. The writer is still in charge when making decisions about how to sound formal and objective. You might say to the writer, "Let's talk about options for sounding formal." Look at passages from handbooks and essays that model effective formal writing and notice specific patterns that create the style that some scholars call the language of the academy.

When working with assignments that seem to call for a restricted voice and style, keep in mind that the main goal is to help writers succeed, not just with one essay, but with college in general. Talking about conventions in stylistic choices also helps students prepare for professional writing in any field. I tell all my students, no matter what their majors, that they are going to have to think of themselves as professional writers throughout college and in their careers. With the emphasis on writing across the disciplines in so many colleges, students have to get ready quickly for discovering, understanding, and using different writing styles relevant to their line of study.

Diversity in writing conventions across fields makes it imperative that tutors help students write for many purposes and audiences. As I've listened more and more to faculty in disciplines other than English, I've learned why some expect a less personal writing style, particularly in upper-level courses. In some cases, scientific writers strive for clarity, simplicity, and brevity by cutting out narratives and descriptions because the journals they publish in have severe space restrictions and the editors must publish as much new research as possible in every issue. When they ask their students to write reports objectively, they are preparing them to develop specific critical thinking skills for their disciplines and to write as professionals in their fields. When writers recognize, with your assistance, that every choice they make is part of their career development, they have another reason for being in charge of their work. In all writing contexts, the writer holds the ownership key in terms of style, and tutors help students use that key by talking about choice and voice. When you help writers discover their stylistic consciousness you are also helping them build and become part of a community of language users that understands how freedom and writing go hand in hand.

Further Reading

Annas, Pamela J. April 1985. "Style as Politics: A Feminist Approach to the Teaching of Writing." *College English* 47 (4): 360–71.

Annas argues for an approach to teaching writing that has women "spend some time learning their mother tongue." She describes her own college course that focuses on bringing together the personal and the political, the private and the public into a risky, experimental style. Her ideas are useful for tutors who are considering ways to encourage women writers to experiment and to value their own voices.

Belenky, Mary Field, Blythe McVicker Clincy, Nancy Rule Goldberger, and Jill Mattuck Tarule. 1986. *Women's Ways of Knowing: The Development of Self, Voice, and Mind.* New York: Basic.

In this major, well-respected study of how women make sense of the world and talk about their understandings, the authors illustrate unique features of women's cognitive strategies and language. Based primarily on interviews with women, this study was groundbreaking in its analysis of the relationships among schooling, culture, and cognition for women. Because the authors were interested in women's voices for this study, their work offers insights into how language, gender, and culture are intertwined (see Sanborn below).

Gibson, Walker. 1966. *Tough, Sweet, and Stuffy: An Essay on Modern American Prose Styles.* Bloomington, IN: Indiana University Press.

A modern classic about style in American prose that will show tutors how American writers use one of these three typical voices that reflect our culture, values, and identity.

Jones, Dan. 1998. *Technical Writing Style.* Needham Heights, MA: Allyn and Bacon.

This text was written specifically for technical writing courses, but it has the clearest and most thorough discussion of style, including a good review of the history of style, that I have found. Tutors will find the definitions and examples to be extremely helpful for understanding choices in style, and the exercises and applications are interesting and relevant to all kinds of writing.

Romano, Tom. 1995. *Writing with Passion: Life Stories, Multiple Genres.* Portsmouth. NH: Heinemann Boynton/Cook.

In this textbook, Romano weaves together his own stories, students' stories, and the multigenre research essay to show how passion can make writing powerful. You'll find good examples here of powerful voices connected to narrative structure in chapters with titles such as "Truth Through Narrative," "Faith and Fearlessness," and "Breaking the Rules in Style." The examples in this book will inspire writers to take risks with their voices and passion.

Sanborn, Jean. 1992. "The Academic Essay: A Feminist View in Student Voices." *Gender Issues in the Teaching of English.* Eds. Nancy Mellin McCracken and Bruce C. Appleby, 142–60. Portsmouth, NH: Boynton/Cook.

Sanborn argues for pluralism in the way teachers assign writing and assess voice and structure. This essay applies *Women's Ways of Knowing* to student responses to their writing processes, and suggests ways to move writers past their blocks that might be a result of a conflict between the teacher's expectations and the writer's natural mode of thinking.

Notes

1. Donna Hickey, *Developing a Written Voice* (Mountain View, CA: Mayfield Publishing, 1993), 1.

2. Hickey, 1

3. Winston Weathers, "Teaching Style: A Possible Anatomy." *College Composition and Communication* 21 (May 1970): 144–49. Reproduced in Tate et al., 295.

4. Wendy Bishop, ed., *Elements of Alternate Style* (Portsmouth, NH: Heinemann Boynton/Cook, 1997), 4.

5. Elizabeth Rankin, "Revitalizing Style: Toward a New Theory of Pedagogy." *Freshman English News* 14 (Spring 1985): 307. Reproduced in Tate et al., 307.

6. See Lennis Polnac, Lyman Grant, and Tom Cameron, *Common Sense: A Handbook and Guide for Writers* (NY: Prentice Hall, 1999).

7. A good book for this is *Sentence Composing for College* by Don Killgallon, which helps students to imitate the sentence styles of professional writers.

Works Cited

Bishop, W. 1997. "Alternate Styles for Who, What, and Why? Some Introductions to *Elements of Alternate Style: Essays on Writing and Revision*" (including an e-mail interview with Winston Weathers). In *Elements of Alternate Style,* ed. Wendy Bishop, 3–9. Portsmouth, NH: Heinemann Boynton/Cook.

Bishop, W., ed., 1997. *Elements of Alternate Style.* Portsmouth, NH: Heinemann Boynton/Cook.

Hickey, D. 1993. *Developing a Written Voice.* Mountain View, CA: Mayfield Publishing.

Killgallon, D. 1998. *Sentence Composing for College.* Portsmouth, NH: Heinemann Boynton-Cook.

Polnac, L., L. Grant, and T. Cameron. 1999. *Common Sense: A Handbook and Guide for Writers.* New York: Prentice Hall.

Rankin, E. Spring 1985. "Revitalizing Style: Toward a New Theory of Pedagogy." *Freshman English News* 14: 8–13. Reproduced in Tate et al., 300–09.

Tate, G., E. Corbett, and N. Myers. 1994. *The Writing Teacher's Sourcebook.* New York: Oxford University Press.

Weathers, W. May 1970. "Teaching Style: A Possible Anatomy." *College Composition and Communication.* 21: 144–49. Reproduced in Tate et al., 294–99.

Williams, J. 1997. *Ten Lessons in Clarity and Grace,* 5th ed. New York: Longman.

8

Organizing Ideas

Focus Is the Key

Alice L. Trupe

A week after my friend had moved into a great Victorian house, I visited her and found every dish unpacked and in the cupboard, every book, tape, and CD in alphabetical order on a shelf. It looked as though she'd lived there for years. "How do you do it?" I asked in amazement. "I can't concentrate on anything else until I've organized my space," she replied.

My office door opens on chaos every morning. Papers flow from my desk to a table, some overflowing onto the floor, floppy disks vie with coffee mugs for shelf space, and anyone trying to analyze my shelving system for books would be kept guessing a long time. I refer to this as creative chaos, and believe it or not, I can find any book or file when I need it! Does it look like organization? Not to other people, perhaps, but it works for me.

Organization in writing works like this. It comes down to whether or not the reader can find his or her way through it. Readers who can find their way believe the piece is well organized. Readers who lose their way say it's not; and since they cannot usually turn to the writer and ask, "Where's the stapler?" they often just give up or scrawl "org" in the margin of the students' papers. Tutors need to show writers where in the draft they become lost or confused and why; other times they need to help writers who don't yet have a draft to think of an organizational plan to get started.

One student pulls two pages of lists from her backpack and tells a tutor, "I have lots of ideas, but I don't know where to get started." Another student hands the tutor a completed draft and asks for proofreading and editing help. The tutor finds that he can't follow the writer's thinking, that the focus seems to shift paragraph by paragraph and even within paragraphs. What strategies work best to support students whose papers seem to lack focus or whose paragraphs strike us as chaotic? What strategies help students find the key to organizing their ideas?

Some Background

Writing textbooks and handbooks generally recommend that student writers start with a thesis sentence, plan an outline, or cluster ideas.[1] Research into the practices and products of experienced writers, however, suggests that their plans and texts do not emerge the way that this advice suggests. Linda S. Flower and John R. Hayes' cognitive model of the writing process, based on analysis of talk-aloud protocols of writers as they composed, describes experienced writers' behaviors as directed by "a hierarchical network of goals."[2] As experienced writers compose, they generate and revise their goals, as well as translate content into words, through a process of discovery and recursion. Inexperienced writers, by contrast, tend to fall back on plans governed by the classroom assignment. Drawing on Flower and Hayes' findings, tutors can help inexperienced writers articulate specific goals for their writing tasks. As students coordinate their goals for affecting an audience with their thinking about the content, they establish their own guidelines for focus and organization.

Tutors may be surprised to learn that a review of the writing of established professional writers has revealed that organization is not a function of clearly defined topic sentences that control subordinate sentences. As Richard Braddock reports in his landmark article, "The Frequency and Placement of Topic Sentences in Expository Prose," fewer than half the paragraphs in twenty-five essays he examined had topic sentences at all. Why, then, do so many writing texts continue to emphasize the outline and the topic sentence? The advice derives from Alexander Bain's 1866 *English Composition and Rhetoric,* as Francis Christensen points out. He comments on the discrepancy between what composition instructors require student writers to do and what they themselves do as writers: "I doubt that many of us write many paragraphs the way we require our charges to write them or that we could find many paragraphs that exemplify the methods of development or the patterns of movement."[3]

Christensen also suggests that paragraphs develop from the topic sentence through "structurally related sentences,"[4] and he notes that a topic sentence does not always explicitly specify the thesis of the paragraph, that it may be a very short sentence or even a fragment, and that it may even be a question. The point is, he asserts, that the sentence should perform the function of orienting the reader. Similarly, Rich Eden and Ruth Mitchell advise that, since readers' interpretations of a text are shaped by the expectations raised at the beginning of paragraphs, paragraphs should be designed from the perspective of a reader rather than shaped by the context of what the writer must say.

W. Ross Winterowd, another rhetorician, argues for a theory of paragraph development based on coherence. The structure of an essay involves transitional relationships between its parts, he believes.

Yet another rhetorician, Frank J. D'Angelo, "revisits" the topic sentence to rethink its usefulness in guiding readers through a text. Citing readability research, D'Angelo makes a qualified argument for the use of "a clearly defined organizational pattern . . . appropriately signaled to the reader."[5] While acknowledging that many texts by professional writers lack topic sentences, he asks us to consider whether those texts might be improved by their use.

Karen Burke LeFevre, who has enriched our understanding of focus and organization by emphasizing the social dimension of writing, observes that each act of invention occurs within a specific social and cultural context, reaffirming the point that writers need to have audience awareness in planning, composing, and revising. This renewed emphasis on audience and context, originating in classical rhetorical instruction, has been blended with the cognitive model in Linda Flower and colleagues' later work, such as her 1994 book, *Making Thinking Visible.*

In short, the message for tutors is that the problem of establishing focus through a clear organizational pattern is best addressed by helping the writer to think through her goals for the text, instead of concentrating single mindedly on meeting teacher explanations or getting everything she knows about the topic into an outline.

What to Do

For either the student who has lists of ideas but does not know where to begin or the student who is ready to revise but whose paper seems to lack a clear focus and structure, the task is twofold: Establish a governing purpose for the text, and organize the text to fulfill the writer's purpose.

Establishing a Focus for the Writing Task

Linda Flower recommends that the student writer "nutshell" her ideas, and this is a useful strategy for beginning discussion: "Tell me, in a nutshell, what your paper is about."[6] Alternatively, the tutor might ask the student to imagine a phone conversation with a parent, a sibling, or a friend back home in which she is telling that person what the paper is about. Another useful scenario involves imagining the paper as a brief e-mail message: "What's the subject line? What can you say in two or three sentences that captures the entire paper in a nutshell?" Having a repertoire of strategies for capturing the gist of the paper is useful for working with writers in either the predrafting or revising phase.

But the writer may need to articulate his goals before getting to a nutshell version of the paper, and this may be especially useful for someone who has not yet started drafting. The way that this writer can establish a structure for his paper is to establish some goals for communicating with the reader. It can be beneficial for tutors to think theoretically about how writers develop goals. While I don't believe writers need to be taught this theory, it does give tutors a framework for understanding and talking about a nebulous but important aspect of teaching writing. In establishing goals, for example, he is doing more than creating an outline: he is creating principles to guide his process as well as his content. Think of these process goals as the instructions people give themselves like, "I want my ending to circle back to my introduction." As Flower and Hayes observe, "Good writers often give themselves many such instructions and seem to have greater conscious control over their own processes than the poorer writers we have studied."[7] They define content goals and plans as "all the things the writer wants to say or do to an audience," and they point out that goals for organization may specify both process and content, as in, "I want to open with a statement about political views."[8] Thus, by focusing the writer's attention on his goals for the paper rather than on a thesis and major points, a tutor may help the writer adopt more effective writing behaviors. And these behaviors can then result in ideas that are more thoroughly developed through a process of discovery. A writer may find it useful to freewrite about her purpose for five minutes or so before creating a tentative plan for the paper.

Planning Reader-Based Rather Than Writer-Based Texts

Some of the most effective growth writers experience comes from shifting their orientation from "What do I want to say?" to "What does the reader need to know?" To plan a reader-based text, tutors can help guide the writer to generate questions a reader might have about the topic. The writer can then draft the text as answers to those questions, revising the questions out of the text at a later stage. Tutors might help the writer to re-enter one of the scenarios suggested above—imagining a telephone conversation and what questions the caller might have, or imagining an e-mail exchange in which someone asks a series of questions based on the previous e-mail message that described the topic in two or three sentences.

An important consideration for tutors to bear in mind here is that while a question-based conversation may seem analogous to the journalist's five "W-questions," the approach I'm suggesting requires contextually based questions, that is, questions specifically connected to the writer's goals for the text. Reducing the questions to a formula like Who? What? Where? When? Why? may reduce the options the writer can imagine for developing her text by focusing all of her attention on telling what she knows, as I mentioned in the previous section.

When a writer has a completed draft that seems disorganized, establishing his goals for the paper may help in rethinking the organization. Articulating the paper's overall purpose in terms of how he wants readers to respond will aid in establishing a rhetorical purpose for deciding what should come first and what should follow each idea throughout the paper. The tutor who plays the role of naive reader by periodically posing questions framed in terms of reader expectations can be very helpful here: "When I read this sentence, it leads me to expect that you're going to talk about X, but then when I get to this sentence, it's not about X, it's about Y, so I feel lost."

Viewing a Confusing Paper as a Discovery Draft

In many cases, a reader has difficulty following a paper because it reflects what the writer thinks he is supposed to do rather than reflecting a rhetorical purpose of his own. Or perhaps the writer has simply transcribed all the information he had on the topic. Either way, the writer hasn't established her own purpose as a writer.

An apparently disorganized paper might actually be a discovery draft, although the student hasn't realized this and so comes to the writing center just to clean up his sentence structure and mechanics. While reading the draft, the tutor finds that the writer has "hit her stride" about midway through the paper, where voice and coherence seems to improve significantly. As a composition instructor, I often see this pattern in papers that students turn in to me. Or perhaps the writer has made her most important point midway through the paper but has retreated from it in attempting to match the conclusion to an introductory paragraph written days ago. In this case, the writer may have started with a very clear thesis statement and written a conclusion designed to match it, all the while overlooking the really important ideas that the writing process itself generated. Such a writer may benefit most from hearing a tutor say,

> Your most interesting point seems sort of "buried" in the next-to-last sentence of paragraph three. It's a good idea. I wonder if it might be easier for a reader to see its importance if you brought it out more. Could you add something to your intro that anticipates this great insight? Will that change your conclusion at all?

The tutor who values the writer's insights and helps her think about organizational patterns that bring them out can experience a tremendous sense of accomplishment.

A writer who discovers what he has to say only in his concluding paragraph will probably benefit most from writing a whole new draft. He, too, needs a tutor's assurance that he has generated good ideas in what he has done so far. The tutor can say,

> It seems to me that your final couple of paragraphs say some really interesting things, and the writing strikes me as stronger here. You could build a whole essay around what you've said here. What would happen if you just started your paper with these two paragraphs and went from there?

When tutors cannot recognize the student's intended organization, outlining the paper is a good first step. The tutor might say, "I think you have some really good ideas here, but I'm having a little difficulty seeing how they fit together. Could we make an outline to look more closely at your organization?" Or mapping the main ideas and creating a visual representation of their relationships can aid the writer in revising for clearer organization. Outlining or mapping at this stage, face to face with a reader, the writer can better see the relationships she has and hasn't established between paragraphs and between sentences (see Macauley, this volume). As she analyzes her own text, she may discover other ways to support her goals for the paper. Remember, outlining need not lead to the creation of a topic sentence for each paragraph; it is, rather, a discovery tool, a technique for discovering what she has to say through looking at how she has said it. "How can I know what I mean until I see what I say?" is the question quoted by Flower, Murray, and other writing teachers.

Using Transitions to Clarify Organization

Using or omitting transitional wording can direct the writer's attention to organizational matters, as Winterowd recommends. A tutor may ask the writer how each sentence relates to the sentence that precedes it and how each paragraph relates to the preceding paragraph. The tutor may help a visual thinker by using the term "signposting" and telling the writer, "Your reader needs directional signs when she arrives at a crossroads." Or the tutor may suggest potential relationships: "Is X an example of Y?" Some words and phrases for introducing examples are *for instance, for example, in some cases,* and so forth. With this technique, the writer may become better able to revise for organization on her own.

Complicating Matters

It would seem as though organization is simply a matter of creating readers' expectations and then fulfilling them, of being predictable. Is there anything wrong with this picture of good writing? Doesn't it sound a little boring? Surely, good writing is anything but boring!

Where's the room for the unexpected, for the surprising? Sometimes a writer's seemingly well-structured text is so predictable that even the reader who holds the grade book will find it boring. Can we encourage such a writer to back off from predictability? Instead of helping the writer to lay out the thesis sentence in the first paragraph, to follow through with several paragraphs headed by clear topic sentences, and to sum up the entire paper in the conclusion, we may need to help her complicate her own template for good writing.

Faced with a predictable text, the tutor might ask the student to talk about the kinds of texts she likes to read (see Masiello, this volume). Chances are that she will mention some popular fiction that captures readers with suspense. A tutor's response might be,

> What is it that you like about Mary Higgins Clark's writing? Are there some
> ways you can use her style of writing as a model for your own writing? Try
> thinking like Mary Higgins Clark. How would she write this paper?

Of course, we're going to temper this line of reasoning with some of the important differences between best-selling suspense novels and classroom writing assignments, but the student who has always divorced her writing from the reading she enjoys may profit from shifting her point of view and thinking of herself as a real *writer*. Students who rarely read for pleasure may especially benefit from this approach if it is expanded to include the song lyrics or the movies they enjoy.

Too often when we read we are blind to our own preconceptions as to what constitutes good organization. It's best to read student writers' texts with open minds. Asking ourselves—and the writer—"What is this writer trying to do here? What are the goals for this piece of writing?" may help us recognize unfamiliar organizational patterns where our preconceived ideas might have obscured the writer's purpose from us.[9]

We may encounter plans that reflect cultural patterns of discourse different from our own, for example. Rhetorical conventions among some Native American tribes, for instance, rely heavily on the establishment of *ethos* (see Masiello, this volume). When a reader accustomed to mainstream academic discourse encounters the text of a writer steeped in these rhetorical patterns, she may judge the text to be too heavily narrative and writer centered, rather than argumentative or expository and reader centered. When the tutor asks the writer to help her as she tries to understand her own goals and plans for what she has written, she may discover sound reasons for his writing in a manner that seems rambling. Then she can affirm the writer's identification with his cultural tradition as well as communicate her response to the text as a piece of academic discourse.

Reading with an open mind means reading student texts from the same stance with which we approach professional and published literary texts. When we encounter writing like James Joyce's *Ulysses* or Dylan Thomas' "Altarwise by Owlight," for example, our question is, "Why did the author do this, rather than that?" If we were to read these same texts in the way we frequently read student texts, our questions might instead sound something like, "Where did this sentence or paragraph go wrong? Where are the topic sentences?"

Some texts have a place for everything and everything in its place, while others work by surprise. The tutor's key to focus lies in helping writers to articulate their purposes and goals, helping them to become more self-reflexive through offering our services as thoughtful readers and responders to their texts.

Further Reading

Connor, Ulla. 1996. *Contrastive Rhetoric: Cross-cultural Aspects of Second-Language Writing*. New York: Cambridge University Press.

Connor draws on research in ESL/EFL writing to discuss the theory of contrastive rhetoric, which has implications for understanding the link between organization in writing and culture (see Ritter, this volume). Using a variety of genres and styles from several first languages, she shows how deeply embedded writing is in culture. Her discussion of the pedagogical implications of this research is valuable for tutors working with native speakers of English as well as for tutors and instructors of ESL/EFL students.

Lawson, Bruce, Susan Sterr Ryan, and W. Ross Winterowd, eds. 1989. *Encountering Student Texts: Interpretive Issues in Reading Student Writing.* Urbana, IL: National Council of Teachers of English.

This collection of essays relates interpretive theory to the practice of reading student writing. Chapters by Janice M. Lauer, "Interpreting Student Writing," and Sharon Crowley, "On Intention in Student Texts," are relevant to understanding how tutors construct a text's organization.

Owen, Derek. 1994. *Resisting Writings (and the Boundaries of Composition).* Dallas: Southern Methodist University Press.

Tutors will be interested in reading Owen's challenge to the teaching of academic discourse as an ethnocentric ideology. He validates a variety of competing rhetorics by quoting from published texts that resist conventional genre definitions. His proposed alternative writing program invites students to practice a variety of styles and genres.

Notes

1. This is a strategy advocated by Gabriele Rico in her text *Writing the Natural Way.*

2. Linda S. Flower and John R. Hayes, "A Cognitive Process Theory of Writing." *College Composition and Communication* 32 (1981): 377.

3. Francis Christensen, "A Generative Rhetoric of the Paragraph." *Notes Toward a New Rhetoric: Six Essays for Teachers.* Reprinted in Francis Christensen (with Bonnijean Christensen), *Notes Toward a New Rhetoric: Nine Essays for Teachers.* (New York: Harper & Row, 1978), 77.

4. Christensen, 79.

5. Frank J. D'Angelo, "The Topic Sentence Revisited." *College Composition and Communication* 37 (1986): 437.

6. Linda Flower, *Problem-Solving Strategies for Writing,* 3rd ed. (New York: Harcourt Brace Jovanovich, 1989), Chapter 7.

7. Flower and Hayes, 377.

8. Flower and Hayes, 377.

9. For an especially good discussion of crosscultural conferencing, see Laurel J. Black, *Between Talk and Teaching* (Logan, Utah: Utah State University Press, 1998), Chapter 4.

Works Cited

Black, L. J. 1998. *Between Talk and Teaching.* Logan, Utah: Utah State University Press.

Braddock, R. 1974. "The Frequency and Placement of Topic Sentences in Expository Prose." *Research in the Teaching of English* 8: 287–302.

Christensen, F. 1967. "A Generative Rhetoric of the Paragraph." *Notes Toward a New Rhetoric: Six Essays for Teachers.* Reprinted in F. Christensen (with Bonnijean Christensen), *Notes Toward a New Rhetoric: Nine Essays for Teachers.* New York: Harper & Row, 1978.

D'Angelo, F. 1986. "The Topic Sentence Revisited." *College Composition and Communication* 37: 431–41.

Eden, R., and R. Mitchell. 1986. "Paragraphing for the Reader." *College Composition and Communication* 37: 416–30.

Flower, L., D. L. Wallace, L. Norris, and R. E. Burnett, eds. 1994. *Making Thinking Visible: Writing, Collaborative Planning, and Classroom Inquiry.* Urbana, IL: National Council of Teachers of English.

Flower, L. 1989. *Problem-Solving Strategies for Writing.* 3rd ed. New York: Harcourt Brace Jovanovich.

Flower, L., and J. Hayes. 1981. "A Cognitive Process Theory of Writing." *College Composition and Communication* 32: 365–87.

LeFevre, K. 1987. *Invention as a Social Act.* Carbondale: Southern Illinois Univiversity Press.

Rico, G. 1983. *Writing the Natural Way.* Los Angeles: Tarcher.

Winterowd, W. 1970. "The Grammar of Coherence." *College English* 31: 328–35.

9

Helping Writers to Write Analytically

Ben Rafoth

One of the challenges tutors face in our writing center is assignments that ask students to analyze something. The instructor might ask for an analysis of the way in which two related readings address an issue or controversy or how a period in history was affected by a specific event. College writers seem to recognize that analysis assignments involve thinking about their topic in certain ways—that it doesn't just mean give opinions or write a description—but they often don't know how to go about thinking and writing analytically for the assignment they have. What they lack, as Muriel Harris points out, is a sense of how it feels to think and write this particular way, and so they seek help from tutors.

Though helping students to think critically and analytically about their assignments is difficult work for even the most talented tutors, writing centers need to be part of this effort. At the same time, the idea that tutors shoulder this responsibility gives pause. Is "help students to think analytically" in anyone's job description? What does it mean for you to help writers in this way? How does a tutor even begin to help students think analytically about their papers, and what are some complications that can arise from this line of work?

Some Background

Before we consider ways to help writers be more analytical in their writing, we first have to look upon writing as a thinking problem, and that necessarily involves entering risky territory. It is easy, though wrong, to make a leap of judgment from a piece of writing to the thinking ability of the writer. The papers students bring to the writing center are snapshots, not movie reels, and they

SEE DISCUSSION TOPIC #5 AT THE END OF THIS BOOK

don't begin to represent the full range of a student's ability. Having said that, the purpose of a writing center is to help students become better and more thoughtful writers. One way tutors can encourage this is by asking students to talk with them about their writing. "Our task must involve engaging students in conversation at as many points in both the writing and the reading process as possible," writes Kenneth Bruffee,[1] who believes that talk is essential to thinking. Bruffee goes on to explain:

> The range, complexity, and subtlety of our thought, its power, the practical and conceptual uses we can put it to . . . result in large measure . . . from the degree to which we have been initiated into what Oakeshott calls the potential "skill and partnership" of human conversation in its public and social form.[2]

In other words, says Bruffee, our thoughts are largely a product of the conversations we have with one another. We can sometimes hear these conversation streams replayed in our minds when struggling with a dilemma, like whether or not to buy a new CD. They are the voices that take us back and forth: "Buy it, you deserve it . . . ," "Save your money, you're going to need it . . . ," "Wait a while and you'll see you don't really want it . . . ," "Oh what the heck. . . ." Bruffee's point is that these subdued voices *are* our thoughts, and they can be enriched by the conversations writers have with tutors, expanding the ways students understand an issue by rendering new intellectual and emotional perspectives or directing their attention to something that has been overlooked.

Helping writers be more analytical in their writing begins with you, the tutor, putting more thought into the way you read and respond. For a writing center to remain committed to the idea of helping writers with ideas, tutors and students must "forge new intellectual partnerships," says David Coogan.[3] The partners must have some knowledge in common for there to be any kind of intellectual relationship, and once this common knowledge is identified you can enter the conversation—not as an all-purpose reader offering generic good advice, but as a specific, individual tutor with particular advice and the occasion to express it. There is no formula for thinking deeper or for the conversation that leads intellectual partners to better writing. As in the game of chess, though, there are plenty of moves that experienced writers use when they have to write analytically, and you can become a more thoughtful responder to student papers by learning some of these moves. They are all around you in the articles and books you are assigned to read in your classes and in the lectures you hear from professors. They appear in newspaper and magazine essays, in debates between experts, and among pundits on television shows like *Meet the Press* and the *Macneil-Lehrer News Hour.* But to recognize them as moves, you have to read or listen with this question in mind: What is the writer or speaker doing, not just saying, to make the points she is making? In other words, you have to assume the writer has a strategy and that it is more than the pure expression of ideas. So, read critically and notice how you are being led, not just from point A to point B, but in a particular way. By enlarging your own awareness of moves, you will become not only a better tutor but a better writer yourself.[4]

For the writers you tutor, you'll need to begin by focusing on the ideas they care about and then stretching them in the give and take of conversation—like making taffy, only not as neat.

What to Do

Every tutoring session needs to revolve around a shared purpose, and this is especially true when working with ideas. What is the purpose of the assignment, and what do you both expect to accomplish in the session? Once agreed, you can use the power of conversation to strengthen the ideas in a paper by examining both your own perspective and the writer's, adding layers of complexity, and using borrowed material to enrich the author's own voice.

Examine perspective   An important idea in our postmodern era is that every person reads and writes from a particular set of perspectives in the culture they belong to. I write as a forty-something English professor and writing center director at a school in rural America, editor of this book, and other perspectives, including many I know more by imagination than direct experience. These perspectives influence how I read and write so that acknowledging where I stand illuminates some of the strengths and limitations of my authority on the subject. It also shows me that what I see comes from how I'm looking and that changing what I see happens only when I change my perspective. This ultimately leads me to think more deeply and critically about my topic, my audience, and myself. As two writing researchers wrote, "Thinking about your positions makes you conscious of the ways you come to know the way you know."[5] Tutors read and students write from perspectives too.

My colleague Lea Masiello tells me that in order to find the ripe green beans in her garden, she has to walk around her garden many times, craning her neck, pushing leaves and branches aside. The ripe ones always hide and to find them you have to keep changing your angle of vision. Reading and writing is like this, too, and so two questions for the tutor to begin with are, How might I step into positions that will give me the perspectives I need for understanding or relating to the student and the paper? and How might I understand things differently if I repositioned myself? If you can reflect openly with the writer about these questions, then she may do the same with you and with the way she looks at her own paper. Actually, this is the kind of conversation that must take place when tutors finds themselves deeply at odds with the ideas in a paper; since there cannot be a dialogue with the writer unless there is common ground, the idea of positioning or taking a perspective can provide some common space.[6]

Imagine, for example, that you were reading a paper on a topic about life in another culture and you found the customs rather bizarre. You might wonder what the writer thinks of these customs and how, given your own feelings, you should respond. Should you express the revulsion you feel about reading of a mutilation ritual? What if the writer gives no inkling of her feelings? Will your reaction prejudice her about her own topic? Or will your reaction make her defensive about the culture she is studying? What I'm suggesting is that you have many avenues open to you, just as the writer does. "As an outsider to this culture, I don't understand why they have these customs, which seem bizarre to me," you might say, "but if I were a member of the culture I would probably have a different opinion about them. I'm wondering what different perspectives you might have." The goal is to help the writer think analytically about the paper by seeing the limits of any single position. At the same time that the writer sees how shifting from one perspective to another generates things to say, you, as the tutor, become a more thoughtful reader of the writer's work as well.

Add complexity to the issue   In most academic writing in the humanities and social sciences that calls for analysis of some issue or controversy, a key move is to define and explain problems, not to solve them. Readers want to feel they have learned something from the reading experience or gained an insight; they usually don't expect the writer to hand them a solution because most prefer instead to seek answers on their own in more indirect ways. When I was growing up, my uncle never wanted to follow the directions my dad gave him to get to our house in the country, so each year he took "a quicker route"—twice as long, but he did it his way. When a writer tries to write analytically, you can help by steering the conversation into exploring the complexity of a subject and teasing out the nature of a problem and its effects. Instead of settling the controversy, this will draw it out, but you'll both probably find that this kind of analyzing is more interesting and engaging than zooming toward some pat answer.

Let's assume the writer has written a draft he is ready to revise and that it has a too-simple thesis and scant development. Bearing in mind the advice above regarding position, you might talk a bit about your response to the paper and the lack of engagement you felt as a reader. You can discuss missed opportunities ("As a humanities major, this part really made me curious about. . . ."), counterpoints ("Because I grew up in a city, this example makes me think of some counterexamples like. . . ."), or point of view ("As somebody who likes to hunt, I understand the gun owners' point of view, but what about other points of view?"). Then work on complicating the thesis statement so that definitions and explanations become central, rather than solutions. Let's see how this might be done with the topic of school violence and its possible relationship to male adolescent depression, something psychologists have been examining recently. Consider this main idea a writer might begin with:

> There are three reasons why male adolescent depression leads to school violence: alienation from peers, distorted sense of reality, and access to weapons.

As the central idea for a paper, this might seem appealing because it's assertive and self-structuring. It says one thing causes another and gives three reasons why. But in fact, it promises so much by way of cause-and-effect relationships that even experts on the subject would shun it. Another approach might look something like this:

> School violence may be related to male adolescent depression, some psychologists argue, while gun control advocates believe that access to weapons is the main factor.

This thesis associates the relationship between depression, violence, and weapons with different perspectives (psychologists, gun control advocates) and it qualifies the claims being made (may be, main factor). It allows for a more complex essay by putting the relationship between these ideas on the table so that the writer can define types of violence that may not be related to depression and explain both the pros and cons of claims. In other words, it tries to put ideas into play rather than nail down the thesis. Once relieved of the burden to defend a hard-to-prove thesis, the conversation you have with the writer can now be about different ways of looking at the issue, the implications that arise from seeing it one way and then another, and the other factors (besides the main one) that might contribute to school violence. In short, once your conversation with the writer has complicated the problem until it feels opened wide up—beyond any hope of a simple solution—the writer is in a better position to examine his idea from multiple perspectives, leaving the reader not with The Solution, which is likely to be inadequate anyway, but with the feeling that a better understanding of the problem has been achieved.

Use outside sources as back-up singers for the author's voice   Aside from showing the professor that the student has read the reading, why do outside sources strengthen a paper? Your writer may need to be reminded why. A professional writer and author of many books about writing, Donald Murray answers the question this way: "Readers are hungry for information. They want images and facts, revealing details and interesting quotations, amazing statistics and insights that make them see, feel and know their world better than they did before the reading."[7] Besides this, I would add, readers enjoy the variety of voices that different sources represent, especially when they are in some form of dialogue with each other. Material integrated from a carefully read article, chapter, or quotation contributes another voice, thereby adding texture to the writing. If you think about it, this is why most singers perform with back-up vocalists, and why we usually prefer listening to a band rather than a soloist. A group contains more interpretations and interactions, making it a more interesting listening experience.

Most writing assignments are related in some way to an assigned reading, which presents an occasion for a different kind of conversation, this time with the ideas of the reading's author. As a tutor, you can help the writer to imagine a dialogue with the reading, like this:

You: The reading says that adolescence is less stressful in traditional cultures than in the West. And you were saying—what was it you said a minute ago?

Writer: Um, I said there probably aren't as many guns in traditional cultures, and that this might be a factor too.

You: Okay, good. Let's go on. The article says that in the West the emphasis on individualism pushes adolescents to become independent, and you say— how would you respond to that?

Writer: (Thinks a while.) Well, I'd say that I can see how this is stressful because parents want to control this independence and that leads to conflict.

As you can see from this dialogue, the tutor helps by drawing out ideas. Instead of skimming the reading for anything he can cut and paste from it, the writer can now follow the thread of an idea with the tutor's help, weaving it between the article and his own thoughts. This kind of dialogue keeps the writer engaged with the reading instead of just plucking quotable quotes from it. At some point you may have to point out that superficial writing tends to be dotted with drop-in quotes and references wherever they'll fit (usually the end of paragraphs). It's a little like name dropping ("As the great Shakespeare once said. . . ."). In-depth, thoughtful writing is more likely to integrate them so tightly that if you tried to remove them, you would almost have to rewrite the entire paragraph. To help writers appreciate how it works, keep an example handy and invite them to remove the quotation and notice how the paragraph falls apart. I tried to illustrate this type of integration with the Donald Murray quote in the first paragraph in this section. I used Murray's words first to answer a question ("Why do outside sources") and then later to make a related point I wanted to include ("Besides this").

Complicating Matters

In this chapter, I have tried to show a few ways you can use conversation to help writers think analytically about their papers. As I was writing this chapter, though, I kept imagining *yes-buts*. Let me share a couple of them with you now.

How much subject-area knowledge must you have before being able to effectively help a writer write analytically? Can you be effective without *any* subject-area knowledge, relying only on common sense? While people who collaborate in the workplace tend to be from the same area or department, writing center tutors tend to work with students on most any assignment in any subject (although some writing centers do have policies on this very matter). This same dilemma faces most composition instructors, whose classes are comprised of students from many different majors, raising again the question of just how discipline-specific writing instruction should be at the college level. There is no easy answer to this, and I think you have to rely on your own good judgment and training to know when you're in over your head. With some topics, that point may come quickly, and you should discuss your limitations with the writer (see Greiner, this volume).

A second complication arises from the fact that helping writers to think analytically does not come easily, and not all tutors in a writing center may be comfortable with the idea of helping students in a way that appears to challenge the ideas a writer is trying to convey. They may agree with a tutor in the Writing Center at IUP who once said he believed that students want tutors who will be supportive of their efforts, not tutors who will complicate them.

But a supportive tutor is not just a cheerleader—he's a constructive critic as well. Ideas, arguments, and values are what writing is about, and students who come to a writing center need a real audience. If the writer's paper seems to lack any kind of analysis or deeper thought, who better to hear it from than a peer? The important thing is how this message is delivered and how supported the writer feels in making the necessary changes. Sometimes writers don't want to change what they've written simply because it took them so long to write it. This is even more reason for you to respond genuinely to the work that students do, because if a student has worked very hard yet produced something that looks as though it was dashed off in twenty minutes, then something is very wrong. For such a writer, the writing center must now become a site of productive tension, a place where thinking and writing analytically begin to create the conflicts that promote growth. It is not the last place of learning for the writer, but it may be the beginning.

Further Reading

Dinitz, Sue, Jean Kiedaisch, and William Mierse. 1997. "Tutor Positioning in Group Sessions." *Writing Lab Newsletter* 21 (5), 11,14.

This article gives tutors some insights into the authoritative and nonauthoritative roles they play when meeting with writers and how the writers perceive these roles. After studying videotapes of actual tutoring sessions, the authors were surprised by the limitations of roles they thought would be effective and the effectiveness of roles they thought would be quite limited. This study is interesting for what it reveals about the perspective that tutors bring to the session.

Flynn, Thomas, and Mary King. 1993. *Dynamics of the Writing Conference*. Urbana, IL: National Council of Teachers of English.

Although this collection of essays is geared more for graduate students and researchers than for undergraduates, it is still recommended reading for anyone interested in investigating relationships between critical thinking and writing conferences. The first chapter, "Promoting Higher Order Thinking Skills in Writing Conferences," is especially helpful.

Kuriloff, Peshe C. 1996. What Discourses Have in Common: Teaching the Transaction Between Writer and Reader. *College Composition and Communication* 47 (4): 485–501.

Written by the director of a writing-across-the-curriculum program, this article addresses a controversy mentioned in this chapter concerning just how discipline-specific writing instruction needs to be at the college level. Do people in one field write all that differently from those in another, or is there common ground that tutors can become familiar with? This article offers some insights.

Notes

1. Kenneth Bruffee, "Collaborative Learning and the 'Conversation of Mankind,'" *College English* 46 (7) (1984): 642.

2. Bruffee, 640.

3. David Coogan, "Email 'Tutoring' as Collaborative Writing," in *Wiring the Center,* ed. Eric H. Hobson (Logan, Utah: Utah State University Press, 1998), 30.

4. Research indicates that expert tutors are self-aware; they reflect on themselves as tutors and writers. See Rafoth, Bennett A. and Erin K. Murphy, "Expertise in Tutoring," *Maryland English Journal* 29 (1) (Fall 1994), 1–9.

5. Elizabeth Chiseri-Strater and Bonnie Stone Sunstein, *FieldWorking* (Upper Saddle River, NJ: Blair Press of Prentice Hall, 1997), 59.

6. While I believe it is important for students to explore the various perspectives they might take, the fact remains that instructors sometimes make it difficult to do this when they make assignments that shoehorn them into choosing from a very limited set of perspectives. The assignment might restrict writers by requiring them to argue for or against one side or the other. Or the restriction might be more subtle, as when an assignment assumes certain values or backgrounds which the students may in fact not share with the instructor. In these cases, I recommend that you continue to explore different perspectives in the tutoring session and then urge the writer to meet with the instructor to discuss why she wants to take a somewhat different approach than what the assignment calls for. At some point, you might wish to read what Marilyn Cooper has to say on the problem of assignments that limit the writer's set of positions.

7. Donald Murray, *The Craft of Revision,* 2nd ed. (New York: Harcourt Brace, 1995), 74.

Works Cited

Bruffee, K. 1984. "Collaborative Learning and the 'Conversation of Mankind,'" *College English* 46 (7): 635–52.

Chiseri-Strater, E., and B. S. Sunstein. 1997. *FieldWorking.* Upper Saddle River, NJ: Blair Press of Prentice Hall.

Coogan, D. 1998. "Email 'Tutoring' as Collaborative Writing." In *Wiring the Center,* ed. E. H. Hobson, 25–43. Logan, Utah: Utah State University Press.

Cooper, M. 1994. "Really Useful Knowledge: A Cultural Studies Agenda for Writing Centers." *The Writing Center Journal* 14 (2), 97–111.

Harris, M. 1995. "Talking in the Middle: Why Writers Need Writing Tutors." *College English* 57 (1), 27–42.

Murray, D. 1995. *The Craft of Revision,* 2nd ed. New York: Harcourt Brace.

Rafoth, B.A., and E. K. Murphy. Fall 1994. "Expertise in Tutoring." *Maryland English Journal* 29 (1), 1–9.

10

Tutoring in Unfamiliar Subjects

Alexis Greiner

Writing centers are asked to help students with papers on topics ranging from bouillabaisse to Brazil nuts. While it may seem advantageous to everyone if the writing center staff included someone from every major, this is not realistic or even necessarily desirable. The fact is, writing center consultants, like most composition instructors, help students from all majors and disciplines learn to write. This is true at Rollins College, where I worked as a writing center tutor, and at most writing centers.

Before going any further, I believe it is important to distinguish between a writing center consultant, the term used at Rollins and the one I will use in this chapter, and an *academic tutor*. At Rollins, we consider a *tutor* to be someone who helps a student with subject matter, while a writing center consultant does not share this goal. Consultants help by provoking thought through conversation, posing questions, and engaging writers in the work of writing. A consultant also helps by urging the student to write because the act of writing is itself a valuable way for writers to discover what they do and do not know about their topic and to figure out what they want to say in their papers. If you are reading this book, you are probably what we at Rollins call a consultant.

How can a consultant majoring in a field such as communication help a student who is writing a paper on a topic like finitely quantifiable abstractions in calculus? At some point, every consultant must recognize when the knowledge gap is too wide and the writer needs to be referred back to the professor for help. The knowledge gap can be a problem even when the consultant and writer are in the same field. Extreme cases are the exception, however, and most of the time tutors can be helpful to writers even when they do not share the same background knowledge on a topic.

SEE DISCUSSION TOPIC #5 AT THE END OF THIS BOOK

Rollins is a liberal arts school where cross-disciplinary writing is an important aspect of the curriculum. By placing our focus more on writing aspects than on the content or subject matter, we are able to use a similar approach with most papers. This makes it possible to fulfill our mission of helping writers across the broad spectrum of the curriculum.

Some Background

Most literature on writing and writing center theory discusses feedback and conversation, the crux of consulting on a paper you know little about. Peter Elbow details two kinds of feedback: criterion based and reader based. The first helps the writer to assess content, thesis, organization, effectiveness of language, and diction. Student writers are most accustomed to criterion-based feedback. Reader-based feedback, on the other hand, leaves the technical stuff behind while the reader expresses the *experience* they gain from reading. Both are useful, but they are applicable in different ways, and at different stages.

Reader-based feedback is a great way to approach unfamiliar matters because it says to the reader, "Look, this is not my field, but your tone and flow reached me through the difficult vocabulary." Or, "The vocabulary you use is specific and difficult, and your writing needs to be super clear to compensate. I feel confused." In such circumstances it is useful to ask clients to assume a reader's role and try to distance themselves from their own writing—so that they can view the paper from a perspective different from their own. This, as Donald Murray says, is in the spirit of teaching students to teach themselves.

What to Do?

In the Rollins Writing Center, like most writing centers, consultants approach each paper in a top-down manner, meaning that we move from a global to a local assessment (see Young; Macauley, this volume). Here is a sample from a consultation with a client I'll call Ann. First of all, notice how Ann responds to my question about the assignment.

Meeting and Assignment

Me: . . . okay, then, let's get started. What is the assignment?

Ann: Well, I wrote a paper on quantum physics and the nature of the protein RNA synthetase and then connected the ideas.

Instead of describing the assignment, which would require her to take her instructor's point of view, Ann tells me what she wrote her paper on. But the two may or may not match, and an experienced consultant knows that now is a good time for a reality check. Ask the client to read the assignment aloud, or at least to consider how her paper does what the assignment asks. (In this example, it turns out that Ann's paper has followed the assignment.) Next, look for key points.

Review Drafting and Pick Out One or Two Key Points

Me: Okay. What have you done so far?

Ann: I have written two drafts and now I am trying to get it into a clearer shape to turn in.

Me: All right, could you, in a sentence maybe, tell me what the connection is that you have found between the ideas?

Ann: I'll try. During cell reproduction there is an interaction between proteins that are affected by laws of quantum physics. I think that is the key to the whole thing.

Me: It sounds like "affected" is a key term. Would you agree? (Ann agrees.) What exactly do you mean by "affected"? I ask because its meaning might be the focus of your paper.

Ann: Well, some of the protein behavior is limited, and some of it is made possible by these laws. And yes, I think that is the focus.

Me: You seem to have a clear grasp on the basics of your idea. Which is a good thing, because it's Greek to me! Let me ask you something else before I read it. Are you comfortable with the organization of your ideas?

Notice how the tutor (me) tries to pick up on things the writer says to help focus attention on what seem like key points. Also, notice how the tutor depends on Ann to confirm what the tutor thinks Ann is getting at. Let's continue.

Read with a Focus

Ann: Yeah, pretty much. I am more used to writing straightforward lab reports, but this is a little different. I wrote it as an essay for a journal, so I modified the structure to include an abstract and then all the rest of it is like a big discussion of the results.

Me: Good. I'll go ahead and read through it now, and I'll focus on the clarity of "affected" and the other things you've told me, and we'll work from there, okay?

Ann: Sounds good.

All consulting is about discovery through conversation, and this situation is no different. If consultants do not know the subject matter, they can use their own curiosity to draw ideas out of the client. By asking the writer to explain what he knows and to view the paper from a distance, the consultant can help the client use his own knowledge to greater advantage in the writing process.

In my experience and those of other consultants at Rollins, the most commonly noted problem is that the work needs better clarity, usually at the paragraph and sentence level, through improved style and diction. If I notice this in Ann's paper, I do not say it immediately. First I engage her in conversation about what she has written.

Test Out Ideas

Me: Ann, I took this sentence here to be your thesis.

Ann: Good—that was my intention.

Me: And then I thought that you used the following paragraphs to support your thesis. Real quickly, I'd like to go through each paragraph and tell you what I got from it in a nutshell. Again, this is not my area, so if I miss something I want you to tell me.

Then,

Ask Thought-Provoking Questions and Build on the Client's Response

Me: This is hard for me to understand. It seems like you are putting forth a formula and then you explain why it works in those reactions. Is that right?

Ann: Close, but not really. I was trying to illustrate a flaw in a fairly well-known theorem as it applies to intercellular interactions.

Me: Ahh. Okay, you could make that really clearer to me by introducing the flaw—"A well-known theorem that has held true in some cases does not in this one . . ."—and so on.

Ann: Oh yeah. That's a good idea.

Me: Go ahead and write, if you want. I'll wait.

I try to establish a pattern that adheres closely to the writer's text and work on that rather than getting into a discussion about general principles of organization, which may not apply in this case (see Trupe, this volume).

There are many ways to make the consultation valuable by relying on your skills at conversation. Be confident in your ability to provide feedback the writer can use. Remember, too, that the client knows that you are not in her field and you can remind her to take this into account when hearing your feedback. If you are still unsure about what to say to the writer or how to be helpful, be frank about your doubts and let the writer tell you what kind of feedback she feels would be most productive—asking thought-provoking questions, perhaps, or working on specific aspects that may be subject-independent or quasi-independent, like organization, tone, diction, sentence structure, and flow. Be confident of your ability to reach a mutual understanding with the writer.

Complicating Matters

Probably the most important thing to be concerned about when working with a client on an unfamiliar topic is to be sure that she understands the limits of your background knowledge and to be sure that you are both in agreement on how best to approach the paper. By explaining your limitations, you ensure that the client is informed about what she can expect from her visit to the writing center, and by agreeing on the approach you ensure a good chance for bringing what you have to offer as close as possible to what she needs.

When reading in an unfamiliar area, it is easy to feel put off by the language and even the tone of the work. It may sound jargon filled and be frustrating to read and follow. While these responses are natural, it is important to trust the writer's instincts and not try to change the writing to reflect your sense of how an essay should sound. This is important because your client probably has a better sense of the writing in her discipline than you do, yet she may not yet fully trust her own instincts and might yield to your advice as the "writing expert." In short, if you cannot articulate a reason for why you think something should be changed, leave it alone, and trust the client's ear over your own about how the paper sounds.

Finally, as a way of learning about writing standards in different disciplines, I recommend inviting faculty from those disciplines to writing center staff meetings, especially if they tend to refer their students to the writing center a lot. Keeping a diverse staff of tutors helps, too. In the end, though, it all comes down to just you and the student, maybe even someone with a paper on finitely quantifiable abstractions. Try to understand the paper as best you can, be frank about your limitations, and build on ideas the writer brings up in conversation.

Further Reading

Blair, Catherine Pastore. April 1988. "Only One of the Voices: Dialogic Writing Across the Curriculum." *College English* 50: 383–89.

If your school has a writing across the curriculum program, this article may be of interest. Many supporters of WAC suggest that each academic discipline has its own way of using language, which can be understood only in its own disciplinary context. Tutors will be interested in Blair's argument that the discipline of English knows only its own way of using language, not all the others, and does not provide an all-purpose academic discourse. So, Blair says, there is no reason for all writing instruction to be taught by the English department faculty. A WAC program should be taught instead by faculty from all disciplines. One possible implication of Blair's article is that tutors can at best know only the discourse of their own disciplines—a different perspective than the one I offer in this chapter.

Clark, Irene Lurkis. 1998. *Writing in the Center,* 3rd ed. Dubuque, IA: Kendall/Hunt.

Chapter 4 of this book, "Interpreting Assignments, Developing Ideas," gives tutors many practical suggestions that can be applied to working with topics that are unfamiliar to the tutor.

Kennedy, Mary Lynch, William J. Kennedy, and Hadley M. Smith. 1999. *Writing in the Disciplines,* 4th ed. Upper Saddle River, NJ: Prentice Hall.

This is one of a number of recent books that deals with the different standards and conventions for writing in the sciences, humanities, and social sciences. Another is *The Harcourt Brace Guide to Writing in the Disciplines* by Patrick Bizzaro and Robert W. Jones (1997). Though not a substitute for the knowledge about writing that someone in the field has, books like this are a good reference to keep on the shelf in your writing center.

Works Cited

Elbow, P. 1998. *Writing with Power,* 2nd ed. New York: Oxford University Press.

Murray, D. 1985. *A Writer Teaches Writing,* 2nd ed. Boston: Houghton Mifflin.

11

Protocols and Process in Online Tutoring

George Cooper, Kara Bui, and Linda Riker

Online writing centers have slowly begun to change the way some writing centers work, enabling students to submit drafts of essays or rough outlines to a writing center tutor via the campus computer network. The most advanced online operations use e-mail attachments, which transmit files directly from a word processing program but can involve compatibility problems. Other online systems rely exclusively on e-mail, which is user-friendly but not very convenient for sending formatted files. In either case, instead of having to visit the writing center, students can get help with their papers from their residence hall or their hometown, eliminating the need to make a trip to the writing center. But does online tutoring change the nature of teaching and learning that has made writing centers so successful? What are some things tutors must know about online tutoring, and how can they make it effective?

Some Background

Collaborative, face-to-face communication has become a hallmark of the work that peer tutors do in campus writing centers. In her essay "Collaboration, Control, and the Idea of a Writing Center," Andrea Lunsford writes about collaboration and how important it is for students to take control of the tutoring situation. She describes a writing center as a place where "knowledge [is] always contextually bound . . . always constructed" and where, in Hanna Arendt's words, "for excellence, the presence of others is required."[1] In *The Practical Tutor,* Emily Meyer and Louise Smith address a similar issue in their chapter "Engaging in Dialogue." They emphasize that conversation is the precursor to development of ideas on paper. Conversation is a familiar aspect of our oral world, and it is necessary for the writer's transition into the written world. In an effort to cultivate the dialogue of conversations, some researchers emphasize the use of opened-ended questions. So important is dialogue that Meyer and Smith include a section entitled "Pace and Tone of Questions," pinpointing the prominent role that dialogue assumes in their notion of good tutoring.

Online tutoring stretches and stresses the viability of these good principles. One could argue that sending a paper online to a tutor can be similar to dropping off dry cleaning—leave your paper at the center on Monday and pick it up on Tuesday with all errors marked and corrected—a practice abhorred in most writing centers. We train our tutors in collaborative learning and see ourselves as facilitators of knowledge, not dictators of it. Not surprisingly, our tutors question whether the success of face-to-face tutoring can be transferred to online tutoring. "How do we engage the student in dialogue when there is really only one of us present at a time?" they ask. "What kinds of questions should we ask to get the writer's attention?" "How can I tell whether the student understands my comments?"

Though principles of face-to-face tutoring do not transfer completely to online tutoring, we can still retain a sense of collaboration and humanity in the online forum. There are online strategies for establishing a relationship between the tutor and writer, for empowering writers to share in their own revision, and for dealing with specifics of grammar and mechanics—all done by relying on collaborative techniques and leading to a facilitated knowledge between tutor and client. As Barbara Monroe writes in "The Look and Feel of the OWL Conference," "Owl [online writing lab], then, is not just an online tutorial service, but a site where meaning and value are shared, contested and negotiated, a site that provokes and promotes new literate practices, both online and in print."[2] Embracing these principles does not solve all problems—and face-to-face tutoring has problems too—but it does result in a shared learning experience. Moreover, we have found that students using our OWL (Online Writing and Learning) service not only benefit from the feedback but even utilize the directed responses more freely, independently, and self-confidently than they sometimes do in face-to-face tutoring. In the section below, we offer some advice, based on an actual online submission and response, for how to make the benefits of online tutoring a reality.

What to Do?

Setting the Right Tone in Introductory Remarks

The writer's first encounter with an online tutor sets the tone for everything that follows. If the tutor's opening remarks are friendly and informal—as they are in the example below with its friendly greeting, contractions, and helpful explanations—the writer will read the tutor's comments as gentle and constructive.

Hi Morton,

I'm Lisa, the OWL tutor who'll be reading your paper. I've read through your questions and will make some notes within your paper about the intro, conclusion, overall structure of your paper and grammar. I'll also try to include major questions I have, as a reader, as I read, so you can get an idea of how an average reader might react. Look for my notes within the body of your paper, set off by asterisks, like this****.

But if the comments are businesslike or formal ("Morton, I read your paper and will make some comments about your introduction"), the writer may hear a harsh and scolding voice, even if the tutor intended otherwise. Written feedback works this way, and keeping the tone lighthearted and friendly is more than a nicety. It is what stands in place of a smile, eye contact, and pleasant voice.

Muriel Harris writes of the importance of this phase of the tutoring session as "Getting Acquainted Time." It is where tutors learn "students' interests and skills, information useful in helping students locate potential subjects for writing."[3] This period of time includes some social and some academic or intellectual engagements. A tutor might begin with small talk about the weather or a detail about the person's dress that sparks conversation. Such small talk is a necessary first-step in establishing trust, and the conversation soon moves toward the student's paper and what kind of help the writer is seeking. The complete process is one which Harris describes as including "getting acquainted time," "diagnostic time," "instructional time," and "evaluation time."[4]

Online Writing and Learning (OWL) environments allow for some of the same processes. Our OWL at the University of Michigan asks students who are submitting papers to include basic facts like their name, year of enrollment, and course, but it also asks students to describe the assignment and to tell what kind of help they want. This provides the same foundation of information needed in any tutoring session.

But because the writer has to type in the assignment and the nature of his request, there is more time to think about what to say, hopefully avoiding "Oh, just check the grammar," which is what students often say when they walk into the writing center and can't think quickly enough, or don't know how to ask for help in any more specific way. Some online writing centers offer students a prioritized checklist of potential problem areas (Transitions, Use of Details, Punctuation, and so on) and ask them to describe the help they seek in each particular area. In this way, it is assured that the student takes the initiative to set the agenda.

Although online comments do tend to get to the point much quicker than face-to-face tutoring, it is important to remember that the online tutor still needs to establish a relationship. By the same token, the writer must describe the assignment and its context as much as possible before the tutor can offer feedback that is genuinely helpful.

Promoting Dialogue in Diagnostic and Instructional Comments

The example below reveals the degree of dialogue that an online conference can generate with a writer.

> ****OK, so your argument is that Reich is generally incorrect in his perception of the impact of foreign workers on the US economy, right? I understand your desire to include in the first paragraph every aspect and detail of his argument, but this is not necessary. In your intro you want to lay out general information about Reich's argument and then set up your thesis, which in this case opposes that argument. Later in your paper you can point by point counter his argument. Also be careful of overwhelming the reader with too many quotes in your intro. While these quotes are probably quite useful to your paper, you can sprinkle them throughout the body of the paper.****

The tutor begins with an opening question, used to summarize what she thinks is the writer's main goal. The question, indeed a rhetorical question, expects no response. Rather, it suggests an openness, a give-and-take between writer and tutor, but surely provides a foundational point of initial discussion. If the tutor gets the topic wrong, the remaining critique and tutorial is undermined. Stated as a question, however, the observation remains negotiable, a misunderstanding possibly due to the reader's interpretation rather than cued by the text. Such possibility provides the writer a common ground with the tutor, an ethos of process shared between them if not entirely a mutual understanding of a piece of writing. The uncertainty expressed in the rhetorical nature of the question indicates the tutor's intention to proceed with an open mind. The next few sentences following the rhetorical question contribute in the way Donald Murray described as "the self proposes, the other self considers"[5] or what Kenneth Bruffee refers to as reflective thought.[6] The tutor's tone is cautionary and invites the writer to reconsider his assumptions about what a good opening approach might be.

In a typical tutoring session peer tutors read a paper aloud, stopping now and then to examine troublesome areas in the text. This puts the tutor in control—and the student on the spot. But the goal for learning theorists who advocate a Socratic approach is to engage the learner, not to manipulate him. Ideally, the tutor asks questions before giving directions and engages the client's own knowledge to solve a problem. In *The Practical Tutor,* Emily Meyer and Louise Smith relate some of the background to this theorizing. They explain writing to be a dialogic process within the mind of the writer, especially the experienced writer. Through conversation, the tutor helps the writer to initiate, recognize, and cultivate the dialogic process used by experienced writers. Online tutors can also use questions to engage writers in this exercise.[7] Because the tutor is not waiting for an answer, the writer is free to act as she wishes. The door to genuine contemplation is open and the writer remains in control.

Questions can serve yet another purpose, and that is to soften criticism. Once again, in the absence of facial expression and voice modulation, the tutor must make points clearly but not coldly, as in this example:

> ****I think that you have explained your opinion well in this paragraph. My only concern for content here is, does a job as a bank teller pay the equivalent as an aerobics instructor? Or does working the line in a factory provide better benefits (i.e., health insurance)? These are things to think about when making very generalized comparisons. Generally aerobics instructors don't work full time nor do they receive health benefits. I understand what it is that you're doing with this example, but I think that the comparison is unfair. Just something to think about.****

This comment occurs later in the paper and works as a probe intended to create dialogue within the writer's mind. In classic fashion, the tutor begins with a compliment before raising a criticism. The criticism is presented as a question, not rhetorical this time but genuine, and, should the writer care to consider it, one which points out a fundamental weakness in the paper: in this case, the writer has made a number of loose, poorly developed correlations. Note the tutor's comment about "when making very generalized comparisons" and how this invites the writer to again share a perspective with the tutor. Here, the tutor has established a foundation for interpretation from which the writer can, by his own will and skill, determine a path of revision. "Well, I'm not trying for very generalized comparisons," he might say. "Why would she say that I'm doing that?" "What does she mean that aerobics instructors don't work full-time? That wasn't my point." And so the dialogue goes. Online tutoring cannot monitor the direction in which the dialogue unfolds or the decisions a writer makes on the basis of it—more on this later. But then, no true collaborator would wish to do that either.

Limiting and Focusing Comments on Grammar and Mechanics

Writing center tutors probably get more requests for help with grammar and mechanics than anything else. What is the best way to respond? Consider this comment from an online tutor:

> ****Two mechanics notes: 1. You want a comma between "agrees" and "explaining," just to make sure the reader doesn't read agreesexplaining, all fast like that. The comma tells the reader to pause. 2. Did you add the word "whom" to Reich's quotation? If so, you should enclose it in [brackets]. (Do that any time you add a word to clarify the meaning of a quotation.) And, because that word represents the subject of a subordinate clause, it should be "who," not "whom."****

In responding online, the tutor has to make a special effort not to correct every error that comes along (see Brooks' "Minimalist Tutoring" for more on this matter; also see Young, this volume). Anyone who has ever seen an online paper that has been meticulously corrected will immediately recognize the problem: with all the insertions of asterisks, question marks, boldface words, and underlines, the paper looks as though it has been worked over. It is ironic that painstakingly correcting every error makes a tutor feel exhausted, while the student who receives the corrected paper feels ashamed. This is not conducive to learning. Comments inserted into the body of the text and set off by asterisks or other marks ($ or % or #) can also seem like litter if they occur too often. On the other hand, e-mail attachment files make it possible to use a word processor like Microsoft Word to insert comments in textboxes or in hidden pop-up boxes and to identify edits with the Track Changes feature or by using a different font color; these look much less intrusive on the page.

Students learn in many ways. Irene Lurkis Clark's essay "Collaboration and Ethics in Writing Center Pedagogy"[8] reminds us that imitation has a long history as a prominent way of learning. Citing Lev Vygotsky, she says that human beings "can imitate a variety of actions that go well beyond the limits of their own capabilities."[9] In the example above, the tutor advises the writer about specific points of grammar and mechanics, correcting and to some degree explaining the logic behind the change. In this example the tutor takes a directive approach and, in its most extreme fashion so far, renders the tutor in the role of proofreader or editor. And yet, the tutor is striking a balance by holding corrections to a minimum (even though there were many other surface errors in this paper) and supplying them with explanation. While this may be no different than it would be when handled in a face-to-face tutoring session, the online forum can do one thing the face-to-face session cannot, and it again involves e-mail attachments. With an attachment, the tutor can insert a hotlink to a Web page that addresses the specific error in question. The writer can then just click on the link and read all about it.[10] (In a face-to-face session, the equivalent would be to tear a page from a handbook and staple it to the writer's draft.)

Consider how another tutor responded to text-level features in the same student's paper. Notice the less directive approach regarding grammar and mechanics:

> ***Also I would like to suggest that you go back and read your paper aloud to yourself. There are a few places where you have pluralized nouns that should be singular or tacked on an "s" to an adjective. These are relatively easy to find when you read through OUT LOUD. Silent skimming does not catch such mistakes, nor does spell check.***

Responding in this way, the tutor recommends the "read aloud" scenario used in face-to-face tutoring. (Note that although the tutor just wanted to emphasize the importance of reading aloud by using all caps, it looks like she is shouting. Our recommendation is, when responding online, AVOID ALL CAPS!) Accompanying the suggestion to read aloud is an indication of what the student might find in doing this, clueing him without telling him directly what to fix. In this way, the tutor avoids the pressure to edit a paper and instead transfers the responsibility of making simple corrections back to the student.

When students submit papers containing many errors, tutors can feel obligated to address each problem as it occurs. This process is time consuming online, pedagogically unsound, and detracts from the tutors' ability to address more global issues. Instead, tutors should locate a pattern of technical errors and use only one or two examples to demonstrate how to correct the problem. In essence, the tutor attempts to teach clients how to recognize and edit errors on their own. In the most severe cases, clients are urged to seek face-to-face help.

Creating Closure with a Final Summation

You will recognize the nature of this end comment (below). Teachers typically write such a remark at the end of a paper. In the online situation, it provides closure to the session.

> ****The overall structure of your paper is good, with ideas flowing from one another. Really what I'd like to see as a reader is more development of your ideas, especially that part at the end about education and gender equality. You can admit that it'll be a difficult transition period, but it's inevitable and in the end will be better than the current situation. I think that's the reaction I was trying to explain when you were talking about aerobics instructors. The paper looks good grammatically; do try to read it over to check for word choice (aboard/abroad) type stuff the spell check can't catch. Good luck with your revisions.****

Murphy and Sherwood say that the concluding stage "contributes to students' feelings of empowerment, providing them with the confidence they need to take the insights they have gained and apply them in new writing situations."[11] In a face-to-face conference this may be done by asking the student to write a brief evaluation note on what the conference accomplished. Online, this task is left to the tutor, but such a closing doesn't attempt to cover everything. The above comment begins by praising what is good about the paper and then reiterates a concern raised earlier about the development of ideas, and in a directive manner it briefly sketches out how the development might unfold. The client should leave this conference as he or she would a face-to-face conference, with a sense of confidence and a solid foundation from which she can proceed into the next draft.

Complicating Matters

Inevitably, the advice we offer above will be complicated by the actual tutoring sessions you will encounter. Whether our advice—or any advice—works or not can only be determined by feedback from the writers themselves, and this can be hard to come by in the online environment. Despite all the strategies tutors use to recreate a dialogue online, one element of conversation remains irrecoverable—body language. Unlike a face-to-face conference, when an OWL tutor sends a finished conference back to a client there is no way to gauge the success of the conference. Harris agrees that "nodding, smiling to show agreement, and offering other small but significant human gestures of friendliness and approval are additional means of conveying our messages" and are important for communication feedback.[12] OWL tutors cannot monitor the client's understanding or receptiveness to their suggestions without such feedback.

Occasionally the tutor has a chance to see the writer's revision. When the tutor examines changes in the revision, the tutor must make assumptions about the motivations behind each change or lack of change. For example, Morton (the writer above) sent our OWL two revisions of his Reich paper, but each version was very similar to the previous one despite requests by three different tutors for more drastic improvements in content, logic, and development. Specifically, the tutors felt that the introduction contained too many quotes, some examples were inappropriate, and his final argument only weakly supported his thesis. The tutors determined that Morton ignored their suggestions for major revisions in favor of the easier sentence-level corrections.

An interview with Morton revealed that he was a very independent writer, looking for feedback more than actual help in writing his paper. He was very concerned with clarity but was confident about what he had to say. According to Morton, one of the OWL's best assets is the opportunity to have more than one person critique the same paper. He anticipated that each tutor would have a different style and would offer different ideas—exactly what he wanted. He ignored the tutors' critiques of his introduction, however, because in class discussions his instructor praised students who used quotes. He did attempt to find better examples for his arguments but said he did not have the time or research skills to find stronger support. As for his concluding argument, Morton felt that he made sufficient changes to clarify that section of his paper. These three OWL conferences combined with his own optimistic opinion of his writing convinced Morton that he would earn an A. His instructor gave him a B−.

Morton was upset and angry. He reported that none of the criticisms his instructor made about the paper coincided with the tutors' comments. She loved his introduction, he said, but she did not feel that his arguments related to his thesis. Overall, Morton did not agree with the teacher's comments or what she felt to be good writing.

From the tutors' points of view, had Morton more carefully considered their comments he might have done better on the paper. Indeed, the fact that the teacher felt the arguments were not related to the thesis indicated to our tutors that they were on to something when they questioned the appropriateness of his reasoning and examples. Moreover, as revealed in the interview, Morton appeared to have been poised from the beginning not to make wholesale changes. His confidence "about what he had to say" may have inured him against really listening (in this case reading) closely what his tutors were telling him. But this is not unique to an online tutorial. Plenty of suggestions are not heard in face-to-face tutoring and plenty of connections are nodded to but not really made. The refusal of a suggestion is perhaps the most significant form of empowerment that a student can make. It might also be argued that online tutoring makes such empowerment even more likely to occur, accompanied as it is by an absence of social pressure.

The most salient aspect of success, if we can draw one from the conference with Morton, has to do with his wanting feedback. He wanted to share in some kind of conversation. Although he claimed that the conferences were too specific to affect his future writing and that to him, the tutors' comments were out of sync with what his teacher wanted, it is not at all clear what will actually unfold as he writes more. He asked for feedback and he got it. Like many students, Morton possessed at this moment a very pragmatic goal—to get a good grade, and that is why he went to our peer tutors. Nonetheless, each tutor had a different (and not-so-different) take on his paper, and he wanted to experience all of them, regardless of whether he chose to internalize or employ this particular advice. Each of us knows from our own experience that human beings sometimes suppress advice and remember it later in life. This, too, is a significant feature of learning; we will learn when we are ready to learn, not before.

More significant than a revision of any one paper is to observe whether or not students continue to submit papers for feedback. (Despite Morton's initial disappointment in his grade, he still sends his papers to our OWL.) Even if our clients do not respond to every suggestion we deem important, they retain their independence as writers to pick and choose how they would like to revise. When clients leave conferences confident enough to take advantage of that independence, when they use the service repeatedly, whether for informal feedback or because they are committed to using the advice they are given, the OWL can maintain and even expand the valuable principles of collaborative teaching and learning.

Further Reading

Coogan, David, ed. 1999. *Electronic Writing Centers.* Stamford, CT: Ablex.

One of the most recent titles on this topic, this book takes the long view of electronic tutoring and what it means for the future of learning to write. The first chapter, Tutors and Computers in Composition Studies, invites us "to look beyond the roles that writing centers have lovingly constructed for the tutor and the writer" so that today's writing centers will continue to be a force in literacy learning in the future.

Dayton, David. 1998. "Technical Editing Online: The Quest for Transparent Technology." *Journal of Technical Writing and Communication* 28 (1): 4–37.

This article will be of interest to online tutors who work with technical papers. The author reviews discussions of online editing in the field of technical communication; he tries to explain how online editing has been shaped within the field and why many technical editors remain loyal to traditional paper-based procedures. Explaining advantages and disadvantages of various software used in online editing, the author reports that online procedures fundamentally change traditional editing. He argues that their use and development is inevitable and ought to be approached both critically and with an open mind.

Harris, Muriel, and Michael Pemberton. 1995. "Online Writing Labs (OWLs): A Taxonomy of Options and Issues." *Computers and Composition* 12 (2): 145–59.

Though now five years old, this article still provides a good overview for understanding some of the most frequently used network technologies available for OWLs. The authors also consider the context for choosing among such a wide range of technologies. They argue that successful OWLs manage to navigate institutional and technological constraints while providing services and upholding sound pedagogical goals.

Hobson, Eric, ed. 1998. *Wiring the Writing Center.* Logan, Utah: Utah State University Press.

A helpful and informative collection of essays that shows the ingenuity and commitment of writing center colleagues as they implement technology in writing classes. Although advocating the use of online technologies in writing centers, the collection also addresses broad and daunting issues of the costs of going online, both economic and pedagogical.

Notes

1. Andrea Lunsford, "Collaboration, Control, and the Idea of a Writing Center," *The Writing Center Journal* 12 (1) (1991): 8.

2. Barbara Monroe, "The Look and Feel of the OWL Conference," in *Wiring the Writing Center,* ed. Eric Hobson (Logan, UT: Utah State University Press, 1998), 23.

3. Muriel Harris, *Teaching One-to-One: The Writing Conference* (Urbana, IL: National Council of Teachers of English, 1986), 41.

4. Harris, 41–43.

5. Donald Murray, "Teaching the Other Self: The Writer's First Reader," *College Composition and Communication* 33 (1982): 140.

6. Kenneth Bruffee, "Collaborative Learning and the 'Conversation of Mankind,'" *College English* 46 (1978): 639.

7. Emily Meyer and Louise Smith, *The Practical Tutor* (Oxford: Oxford University Press, 1987), 31–32.

8. Irene Lurkis Clark, "Collaboration and Ethics in Writing Center Pedagogy" in *The St. Martin's Sourcebook for Writing Tutors,* eds. Christina Murphy and Steve Sherwood (New York: St. Martin's Press), 88.

9. Clark, 92.

10. The Online Writing Center at Indiana University of Pennsylvania is an example of an OWL that uses attachment technology to insert hot links into the student's online paper.

11. Meyer and Smith, 14.

12. Harris, 43.

Works Cited

Brooks, J. 1995. "Minimalist Marking." In *The St. Martin's Sourcebook for Writing Tutors,* eds. C. Murphy and S. Sherwood, 83–87. New York: St. Martin's Press.

Bruffee, K. 1984. "Collaborative Learning and the 'Conversation of Mankind,'" *College English* 46 (7): 635–52.

Clark, I. L. 1995. "Collaboration and Ethics in Writing Center Pedagogy." *The St. Martin's Sourcebook for Writing Tutors,* ed. C. Murphy and S. Sherwood, 88–95. New York: St. Martin's Press.

Harris, M. 1986. *Teaching One-to-One: The Writing Conference.* Urbana, IL: National Council of Teachers of English.

Lunsford, A. 1991. "Collaboration, Control, and the Idea of a Writing Center." *The Writing Center Journal* 12 (1): 3–10.

Monroe, B. 1998. "The Look and Feel of the OWL Conference." In *Wiring the Writing Center,* ed. E. Hobson, 3–24. Logan, UT: Utah State University Press.

Murray, D. 1982. "Teaching the Other Self: The Writer's First Reader." *College Composition and Communication* 33: 140–47.

Murphy, C., and S. Sherwood. 1995. "The Tutoring Process: Exploring Paradigms and Practices." In *The St. Martin's Sourcebook for Writing Tutors,* eds. C. Murphy and S. Sherwood, 1–17. New York: St. Martin's Press.

Meyer, E., and L. Smith. 1987. *The Practical Tutor.* Oxford: Oxford University Press.

12

Recent Developments in Assisting ESL Writers

Jennifer J. Ritter [1]

Experienced writing center tutors are accustomed to working with undergraduate, graduate, traditional, and nontraditional students. We quickly learn to change our approaches to accommodate each student's differences. When working with English as a Second Language (ESL) students, we encounter yet another layer of differences. ESL students bring different cultural backgrounds, writing experiences, and English language proficiency to the English writing context. And because many of us are not trained to tutor writers who are working in a second language, our tutoring instincts may short-circuit.

As a native-English speaker, when I reflect upon my tutoring sessions with ESL students, the main difference that I notice between native-speaker and ESL writing is the language. When we read ESL writing, we see expressions or grammatical forms that sound foreign, like a written foreign accent. Unlike native speakers, ESL students may not have high levels of English language proficiency to fall back on. Faced with these aspects of ESL writing, I find it hard to decide whether or not to work on grammatical forms in the tutoring session. Part of my dilemma stems from the fact that I can usually get the gist of the ESL writer's message, and yet, I wonder whether I should still try to help the writer to revise forms and expressions, like verb endings and idioms. I also wonder whether working on these points of language will benefit the students not only with writing, but also with their learning English. As a graduate student studying second-language acquisition (SLA) and a writing center tutor, I have learned the importance of nonprescriptive negotiated tutoring. But how can negotiation work when there is the added problem of English language proficiency?

Although we are still exploring how we can work best with ESL students, recent research in writing center tutoring and my own field of second language acquisition offers some insights. One insight is that when a tutor and ESL student negotiate meanings and forms in the student's text, the ESL student can improve his or her proficiency in English. This chapter will share the logic behind this idea of negotiated interaction and how we can use it in ESL tutoring conferences using an experience I had when I worked with a 33-year-old Japanese graduate student named Rika (not her real name).

Some Background

When working with Rika and other ESL students in writing conferences, it seems the dynamics of the tutoring too often change from nondirective to directive approaches. In fact, this change is documented by Judith Powers, who noticed that tutor roles shifted from collaborators to informants when they worked with ESL students. Not only does the tutor role shift more towards informant, but, as Cumming and So acknowledge, there is a stronger tendency to correct errors in the ESL students' texts. From the viewpoint of writing center tutors, these types of conferences contradict our beliefs in nondirective tutoring. As Powers says, we need to devise strategies that are both appropriate for ESL writers and more compatible with writing center philosophy.[2]

In a national survey of writing centers, researchers found that the two most frequent differences in conferences involving ESL writers are the writers' concerns with sentence-level correctness and greater expectations of editing.[3] These differences are to be expected when we consider that unlike native speakers, most ESL students do not have complete fluency in English. When learning a second language, it is rare for anyone to reach a native-speaker proficiency level, or ultimate attainment. This means that most ESL students will acquire grammatical aspects of the language to a certain point and may never go beyond that level. Many ESL students, for example, cannot acquire native-speaker proficiency with grammatical forms such as word choice and word order and will say things such as "Almost it is the same tall as the building." The implication here is that native-speaking tutors may have to include more grammar instruction in ESL tutoring conferences since they have knowledge about English, which their ESL students may need but will probably never attain without instruction.

Errors are a natural aspect of ESL writing and even though they make the writing sound foreign, not all of them interfere with reading comprehension. As tutors, then, we should learn how to recognize which ESL errors are more serious and can affect reading comprehension. Global errors affect reading comprehension and can include word choice, relative clauses, and word order.[4] An example of a word choice error appears in a paper that Rika wrote about earthquakes when she described how she tried to protect her home. She wrote, "I leave curtains closed because if glass of the window is broken, the curtains *shoot* down from a piece of glasses into the room." In this sentence, a native speaker might interpret "the curtains *shoot* down" in a couple of ways: "the curtains will fall down because of the breaking glass" or "the curtains will keep the broken glass from flying into the room." Since the word *shoot* makes the meaning of this sentence unclear, this error creates a comprehension problem.

Local errors, on the other hand, include things like articles, prepositions, and pronoun agreement, and they usually do not affect reading comprehension.[5] Article and preposition errors are also some of the most difficult for the second language learner to master. These seemingly simple grammatical forms are also among the most difficult for native speakers to explain. Try explaining, for instance, why English uses the preposition *at* for both "I am at school" and "The party is at seven o'clock." If we say that *at* is used for both place and time, then why do we also say, "I am in school" and "The party is on Sunday"? When it comes to local errors like this, there is not much to negotiate and the best thing is simply to tell the writer which words to use.

We can also draw from second language acquisition research to decide how to work with ESL students on language problems. One theory that can be applied to the writing center tutoring context is the Interaction Hypothesis. One idea behind this hypothesis is that ESL students can learn English through conversation with native speakers.[6] In other words, if the ESL writer's message, whether it be spoken or written, is unclear to the native-speaker tutor, then the two of them can negotiate the meaning of the message. The ESL student, then, is pushed to modify his or her language. Here is an example of negotiated interaction between Rika and me:

Jennifer: So, can you tell me what your paper is about?

Rika: This paper is about earthquakes in Japan. I talk about *evacuating drill* in school.

Jennifer: [initiating negotiation] I am not sure what you mean. Are you talking about an *evacuation* drill where the students and teacher practice for earthquakes?

Rika: [modifying her language] Yes, I talk about evacu . . . evacuation, is that right?

Jennifer: Yeah.

Rika: Okay, it is about evacuation drill. Does it make sense to you?

Jennifer: Yes, it does.

As a result of the negotiation, Rika modified her language.

In sum, writing center tutors must recognize that English language proficiency can be problematic in ESL writing. Where the ESL student needs assistance, in this case, is with native-speaker intuitions about English, which helps to push the ESL student to recognize their errors. Strategies that we can use to accomplish this can be adapted from second language acquisition research that suggests that conversation and negotiation help in correcting language errors.[7] Negotiation not only allows the tutor to understand the message more clearly, it also provides the speaker an opportunity to develop language proficiency. The implication for the writing center context is that we should negotiate both the meaning and the grammatical forms of the text in order to assist ESL students in improving their writing and grammar.

What to Do?

Negotiate the Agenda

We negotiate the agenda with ESL writers as we would with native speakers. We should ask about the student and his writing assignment, beginning with larger rhetorical concerns. The difference, however, is that ESL students will want help with grammatical correctness at some point,[8] and since ESL grammatical errors can affect reading comprehension, these are the errors that should be negotiated during the tutoring session.

Since negotiated interaction, in the sense that it is presented in this chapter, may not seem like a normal conversation, it is helpful for the tutor and ESL writer first to talk about how they will work on language problems. At the beginning of the session when we are learning about the student's needs, we should discuss how best to negotiate. For instance, having the writer read the paper aloud may not work best for him. When a student has a low level of English proficiency, reading aloud may focus attention away from the writing and onto pronunciation, which is not our goal. Rika, for example, felt that she ought to try to read her paper without making any mistakes because errors would be embarrassing for her, even though she knew that the tutor would not mind. But reading aloud may not be an issue with every ESL writer, and we should ask whether they are comfortable reading aloud.

I recommend talking with ESL writers about how to assist them with their grammar. If, for example, you will be reading the paper to the student, you might ask whether they prefer that you pause, repeat, or stress certain words when you notice an error. On the other hand, if the student will be reading the paper aloud, try to devise some other techniques to signal an error. You might raise your hand, point to a word with your pencil eraser, or ask questions. This is how Rika and I negotiated the agenda:

Jennifer: So, Rika, I would like to know if you would like to read your paper to me or if you want me to read your paper to you.

Rika: Can you read it?

Jennifer: Yeah. So, if I am reading it, I need to tell you how I will point out some grammar errors. Listen to me and if you hear me *stress* some words or phrases, or if I just stop reading, I am trying to show you that it doesn't sound right to me. Does this make sense?

Rika: I think so. I will try to listen for this.

Whatever you decide to do, choose techniques you will both be comfortable with. Over time, this type of conversation will seem natural.

Negotiate the Meaning and Form

In ordinary conversation, speakers often negotiate the meaning when misunderstandings arise. With ESL students, these misunderstandings can be a result of language proficiency. As a conversational strategy, negotiating meaning in the writing center conference can help students notice areas that create comprehension problems. For English language proficiency, negotiation of meaning will most likely arise from global errors involving word choice, relative clause, and word order.

We can negotiate the meaning and form of a text when we want to confirm our understanding or when we do not know what the writer meant. When I was working with Rika, for example, I needed to confirm my understanding of her text where she wrote about another precaution she takes against earthquakes. She said, "I turn off the gas if I am using because of a fire." As a native English speaker, I was not exactly sure what Rika was attempting to say, and I tried to slow things down so that she could discover how to clarify the meaning herself.

Rika (reading her paper): I always do when an earthquake strikes. First, I turn off the gas if I am using because of fire.

Jennifer: [initiating negotiation] Hmm, if I am using because of fire?

Rika: Yes, the gas may cause fire.

Jennifer: Oh, so you turn off the gas to *prevent* a fire?

Rika: Is that how to say it? Prevent?

Jennifer: Yeah. If you want to keep something from happening, we use the verb *prevent.*

Rika: How should I write it? First I turn off the gas . . . um . . . prevent fire?

Jennifer: That's close. I turn off the gas *to* prevent a fire.

Rika: Okay. I turn off the gas to prevent fire.

Through negotiating the meaning in this sentence, Rika first realized that she did not know which word to use in this context and then, with help, used the correct form.

If I were reading the paper aloud to Rika, on the other hand, I would try to negotiate the meaning by again slowing things down and emphasizing areas that do not sound right. I might stress certain words or pause at points. If Rika did not realize that I was trying to get her to notice this part of her paper, I would keep repeating the words or phrases and then try to negotiate with her.

Jennifer [reading paper, initiating negotiation]: My family is prepared to precaution . . . *to precaution* for earthquakes. *To precaution?*

Rika: Is something wrong?

Jennifer: This phrase just does not seem to work. My family is prepared to precaution. What do you think?

Rika: I don't need precaution?

Jennifer: Yeah, you just need to say my family is prepared.

Rika: My family is prepared for earthquakes?

Jennifer: Yep. It makes sense just to say my family is prepared for earthquakes.

Again, Rika's problem is language proficiency and she was overgeneralizing the use of the verb *precaution* and used it as a noun. As native speaking tutors, we can help the writer then notice these areas and negotiate how to revise the problem.

Another consideration whenever we are working with ESL students on grammatical form is whether to focus only on global errors or local errors such as articles and prepositions. In general, articles and prepositions do not cause any serious difficulties with reading comprehension and they should not be a high priority for tutors, according to Harris and Silva. When I quickly read Rika's sentence, "Also I leave curtains closed," I understood the meaning and did not immediately notice that there is a missing article. Although it sounds foreign, the error is not serious enough to spend a lot of time helping Rika figure out what is wrong and how to correct it. I would spend time on this error type only if there were no serious errors in her paper.

Online ESL Tutoring: Provide Models

When we treat grammar and language proficiency problems in ESL writing online, we need to model the language forms for the writer. Although online tutoring does not have the convenience of moment-to-moment negotiated interaction, it is still possible to help ESL writers notice and correct language problems. When I notice global errors in an ESL writer's paper, I first respond with my questions about what I think the writer intended to say. Then, I model corrections as in this example:

Rika's text: In serious case such as a big earthquake, students had to leave at the school with teachers until someone from home comes to pick them up.

My Comment: Rika, so, are you saying that (1) the students stay at the school with the teachers until someone comes to pick them up? Or, are you saying that (2) the students leave the school and wait with their teachers somewhere else? If you are saying (1), in English we usually say something like "the students had to *stay* at the school with the teachers." If you are saying (2), we usually say something like "the students had to *leave school with their teachers*." Does this make sense?

With the questions, I am showing Rika that I misunderstood her message with the intention that she notice a language problem in the sentence. I also wrote two possible corrections to provide Rika with a model of the grammar. The emphasized text is used to direct Rika's attention to what I believe is the specific problem, which is her use of the verb *leave*. Providing language models is important for ESL online tutoring because the ESL student may not know how to correct the language when the correction deals with forms they may not have attained yet. (See also Cooper, Bui, Riker, in this volume.)

Complicating Matters

In an ideal world of writing center tutoring, we would be able to follow a few simple steps in each tutoring session that would allow the writer to improve their writing and the tutor to feel a sense of accomplishment. ESL tutoring is no exception. Steps such as negotiating the agenda, meanings, and forms may not always work in a straightforward manner to help the writer improve, however. Here are some problems that you may experience when tutoring ESL students.

You may have the feeling that all the problems in ESL writing stem from language proficiency. This would be an overgeneralization, however, since it does not account for other factors that can affect ESL writing including cultural background and writing abilities. Though it is quite possible that ESL students will need help only with language, as Rika did, this will not always be the case and we should plan to approach each situation with a focus on the student's meaning, discussing matters of grammar as the need arises.

A challenge for any tutor committed to negotiating meaning and form is ensuring that the writer discovers problems on his own. When the ESL student is unaware of language errors due to limited language proficiency, it would be all too easy for us to take a directive role because we have knowledge that the ESL student lacks. The problem, then, is to get the student to notice that the form is incorrect and then to correct it while the tutor remains nondirective. With global errors especially, we want to negotiate because it *slows* the conversation and allows the student more time to process information. In other words, negotiation creates a learning moment. It is not possible to spell out procedures to unfold this process of negotiation. Instead, tutors need to try out different approaches, including the ones described here, and find what works best.

In this chapter, I have presented a way to make the ESL student responsible for their writing while also allowing the tutor to take on the role of informant. Further research in ESL tutoring is needed, however, and writing center tutors are in a good position to conduct this research. For instance, we need to examine how we can address cultural attitudes towards writing that may conflict with American academic writing conventions. (An interesting and useful book on this topic by Helen Fox is listed below.) We also need to explore how we can work most effectively with ESL students during the short time period that we have to work with them. By studying any of these questions, among others, tutors can help to ensure a better fit between ESL tutoring and the nondirective approach of writing centers.

Further Reading

Fox, Helen. 1994. *Listening to the World: Cultural Issues in Academic Writing.* Urbana, IL: National Council of Teachers of English.

The author discusses the difficulties that students from other cultures face in American universities, explaining how cultural values such as indirectness and collectivity make it hard for ESL students to learn U.S. academic writing. This book is useful for any tutor who wishes to learn more about how culture can affect both writing and conferencing. The last chapter, "Helping World Majority Students Make Sense of University Exceptions," is especially helpful for working with cultural issues in tutoring conferences.

Harris, Muriel and Tony Silva. 1993. "Tutoring ESL Students: Issues and Options." *College Composition and Communication* 44: 525–37.

This article is highly recommended for any tutor or writing center director who wants to learn more about tutoring ESL students. Harris and Silva explain some of issues related to ESL writing including error types, cultural preferences in writing, and writing process differences. Harris and Silva also provide tutoring suggestions for these issues.

Severino, Carol. 1993. "The 'Doodles' in Context: Qualifying Claims about Contrastive Rhetoric." *The Writing Center Journal* 14: 44–61.

Contrastive rhetoric is a term in the field of second language acquisition used to describe cultural orientations that writers have towards texts. Severino explains the controversies related to contrastive rhetoric and the implications for ESL tutoring. This article is appropriate for tutors who would like to learn more about contrastive rhetoric and ESL tutoring.

Thonus, Terese. 1993. "Tutors as Teachers: Assisting ESL/EFL Students in the Writing Center." *The Writing Center Journal* 13: 13–26.

Thonus discusses three approaches to teaching and tutoring ESL writing: focus on form, focus on the writer, and focus on the reader, providing examples along with an explanation of the teaching approach. This background information in combination with suggestions for tutoring make this article beneficial for any tutor working with ESL students.

Notes

1. I would like to thank Akiko Suzuka and Yasuko Ono for the useful discussion on ESL tutoring and for providing the ESL writing examples.

2. Judith Powers. "Rethinking Writing Center Conferencing Strategies for the ESL Writer." *The Writing Center Journal* 13 (1993): 40.

3. Judith Powers and Jane Nelson. "L2 Writers and the Writing Center: A National Survey of Writing Center Conferencing at Graduate Institutions." *Journal of Second Language Writing* 4 (1995): 125.

4. Joy Reid. *Grammar in the Composition Classroom.* (Boston: Heinle, 1998), 126. Robert J. Vann, Daisy E. Meyer, and Frederick O. Lorenz. "Error Gravity: A Study of Faculty Opinion of ESL Errors." *TESOL Quarterly* 18 (1984): 432.

5. Reid, 126. Vann et al., 432.

6. Susan Gass, Alison Mackey, and Teresa Pica. "The Role of Input and Interaction in Second Language Acquisition: Introduction to the Special Issue." *The Modern Language Journal* 82 (1998): 302.

7. Gass et al., 302.

8. Muriel Harris and Tony Silva. "Tutoring ESL Students: Issues and Options." *College Composition and Communication* 44 (1993): 533.

Works Cited

Cumming, A., and S. So. 1996. "Tutoring Second Language Text Revision: Does the Approach to Instruction or the Language of Communication Make a Difference?" *Journal of Second Language Writing* 5: 197–226.

Gass, S., A. Mackey, and T. Pica. 1998. "The Role of Input and Interaction in Second Language Acquisition: Introduction to the Special Issue." *The Modern Language Journal* 82: 299–305.

Harris, M., and T. Silva. 1993. "Tutoring ESL Students: Issues and Options." *College Composition and Communication* 44: 525–37.

Powers, J., 1993. "Rethinking Writing Center Conferencing Strategies for the ESL Writer." *The Writing Center Journal* 13: 39–47.

Powers, J., and J. Nelson. 1995. "L2 Writers and the Writing Center: A National Survey of Writing Center Conferencing at Graduate Institutions." *Journal of Second Language Writing* 4: 113–31.

Reid, J. 1998. *Grammar in the Composition Classroom.* Boston: Heinle.

Vann, Robert J., D. Meyer, and F. Lorenz. 1984. "Error Gravity: A Study of Faculty Opinion of ESL Errors." *TESOL Quarterly* 18: 427–40.

13

Can You Proofread This?

Beth Rapp Young [1]

Anyone who works in a writing center becomes familiar with requests like, "My paper is due in 45 minutes—can someone here proofread it for me?" With imposing urgency, some writers expect tutors to give the paper absolution and a quick blessing. Tutors risk disappointing students when they explain that they cannot comb through a paper for errors, mark and correct each one, and hand the paper back with a stamp of approval. There is another kind of risk as well, and this one stems from the very idea of correctness in writing. What's correct? Who is to judge? Why does it matter? Some writing centers try to stay away from proofreading altogether. Yet the fact is, students enter most writing centers expecting to receive help on all aspects of their writing, including final editing. This chapter offers thoughts on why proofreading is a dilemma in itself, and then—for those who struggle with it—some ways to help writers proofread their own papers.

Experienced tutors understand that when writers ask us to proofread, they may really be asking, "What do you think of my ideas?" "Have I supported my point?" or "Does it flow?" Careful questioning is important when working with a writer you've never assisted before. What many tutors don't realize is that the decision to proofread requires a shared understanding between the tutor and writer, one that recognizes the problems inherent in bringing papers to the writing center for proofreading. The first step, therefore, is always to be alert to the possibility that the writer may ask for help with grammar or proofreading when he actually wants something different but doesn't know how to ask for it. So if there is an opportunity to talk about ideas, take it and leave the proofreading for later. After all, once the writer changes the ideas and sentences, proofreading must begin all over again.

What about when the writer says, "I feel very good about the ideas and the organization—I've shown it to other writing consultants and other people in the class, and I've incorporated their suggestions for revision. Plus, this paper is due in an hour. So I need someone to look it over and see if there are any errors."? Should you tell that writer that she has come to the wrong place?

Some would argue that proofreading is against the purpose of writing centers because writing centers are supposed to work towards better writers, not better papers (for a famous example of this dictum, see North). Another argument is that proofreading supports an unrealistic view of writing-as-product, not process. Proofreading does this by ignoring the global revision needs of a paper in favor of error checking, especially when the writer still needs to work on ideas and organization. (Clark compares too-early proofreading to polishing fifty pieces of wood before you know which pieces you'll use to build a table. Obviously, building the table should come before polishing it.)

Finally, some worry that an emphasis on proofreading will transform the experience of working in a writing center. Rather than focusing on the writer, writing consultants will need to focus on the text. Will writing consultants enjoy proofreading as much as the other work? And what if they miss an error or two? Will the writer hold the writing center responsible? Will writers even bother to proofread if they know someone skilled at writing can do it for them? And what message does *that* send? Questions such as these illuminate potential risks associated with proofreading. Each writing center should try to define its own purpose and mission in ways that recognize these risks.

One way to understand proofreading is in terms of the writing process. How can a writing center be complete, providing help from invention to revision, if it doesn't pay full attention to that final step? Arguably, ignoring something that matters to most readers gives an unrealistic view of the writer's obligation to her reader and creates the impression that correctness doesn't matter. Besides, writers learn from modeling. When we say, "We can't proofread for you, but we'll teach you how to proofread your own paper," there is an opportunity here to show the writer how good proofreaders work. Part of the argument for writing centers is that an outside reader can notice things the writer cannot because he or she is too familiar with the paper. Writers can learn from tutors how to step back from the piece and see it with fresh eyes. Finally, let's remember that writers may visit the center for proofreading but return for other kinds of help. Proofreading may just be the entrée.

Some Background

A large body of research on errors and correction in writing provides different perspectives on this issue. While some have tried to classify the different types of errors and determine which ones occur most frequently (Connors and Lunsford), others have examined the effects that various errors have on readers' attitudes (Hull; Hairston). Modern approaches to error have been more inclined to follow Mina Shaughnessy's lead and regard error as a natural part of learning the skill of writing. When viewed this way, errors are not always straightforward mistakes. Sometimes they are the result of an incorrect or misapplied rule that the writer has learned, or they may be caused by intrusions from the writer's spoken language (or her first language, in the case of second-language writers).[2] And sometimes they lie in the eye of the beholder. In an article in the journal *College Composition and Communication,* author Joseph Williams slyly inserted about one hundred errors—typos, misspellings, repetitions, and so on—into his article on error, but few readers (college English teachers mostly) caught on until the author told them at the end what he had done. His purpose was to demonstrate that English teachers find numerous errors in student writing because they are looking for them, and where they do not expect to find them, they don't, even when they are plainly there.

Errors are no joke in most teachers' minds, however, and students are justifiably concerned about the impact that errors will have on their grade. Helping a writer to proofread can be tremendously valuable when it is done for the purpose of teaching the student to find her own errors. Tutors may pride themselves on doing this well. Some writing centers approach the issue as a research problem by first listing all of the errors and then studying them with the writer to see what they have in common. In the long list of possible errors writers make, it is worth noting that readers tend to be bothered more by some than others—usually sentence-level problems (run ons and fragments), excessive commas, and nonparallel constructions (Cazort; Hairston).

What to Do?

Beginning tutors may be tempted to plunge right in, but experienced tutors know that proofreading is rarely a straightforward process. Here are some general strategies to bear in mind. (In the following section, you will see some specific suggestions for helping writers.)

First, talk with the writer about proofreading before you begin it and decide whether it is necessary at this time. If so, be honest about your own limitations and don't allow yourself to be framed as a writing expert; this would be a no-win situation for both of you. It is better to treat the problems you are unsure about as curiosities, and you will be surprised at how often the real answer is that there is no single correct answer. This is not because there are no correct answers. Rather, many of the questions that writers express involve aspects of language usage that have more than one right answer. This is another reason why it is important to understand that proofreading is not a straightforward business and that editing decisions are ultimately the writer's responsibility.

Experienced tutors don't attempt to pick out every mistake they see. Instead, they look for error patterns. You and the writer can then decide which errors to work on. Spelling, for example, might be something the writer feels he can correct on his own or with spell check. Software such as MLA's Editor5 may help with error analysis. Use grammar checkers with caution, though, because they identify many "errors" that aren't errors at all (like passive voice) and they fail to catch errors that really are (like agreement). Look for grammar checkers that print a comprehensive list of errors, rather than requiring you to address each error one at a time. The comprehensive printout can be reassuring because what looks like eighty-five individual errors with a standard grammar checker may turn out to be only four patterns of error. Nonetheless, many writing centers avoid grammar and style checkers altogether because of the mixed messages they can create.

Remember to make errors the writer is most concerned about a priority. You can determine this by asking questions about errors that have been marked in earlier papers, those that seem to be especially annoying to the instructor (sexist language, perhaps), or that will be fatal for that assignment ("any paper with two or more sentence fragments will fail"). For writers worried about questions that have no clear right-or-wrong answers, it may be best to focus on matters of voice, tone, consistency, or purpose as a way of deciding what to do (see Masiello, this volume).

In your discussions, don't be afraid to turn to a handbook! Writers are sometimes unsure about how to use handbooks effectively, so when you turn to a handbook you model an important skill that writers can learn to use on their own. Beginning tutors sometimes worry that consulting a handbook hurts their credibility, but actually, demonstrating that you know how to use writerly resources enhances your credibility at the same time that it helps you resist being framed as the authority. In fact, it's often useful to consult more than one handbook, because different handbooks explain concepts differently, yielding a fuller understanding of the issue. Sometimes handbooks even disagree, and that disagreement can help a writer stop seeking *the* correct answer and start considering which strategy is best for her particular paper. Consulting handbooks is a great way for tutors and writers to learn more about language and how it works.

Finally, I recommend that tutors look for opportunities to learn about language and how it works. Read and write often, paying attention to how authors convey different tones and experimenting with new styles in your own writing (see Bishop; Eckard and Staben, this volume). A heightened sense of curiosity about writing is what many tutors point to when they say that working in the writing center taught them more about writing than they could have learned in any class.

Regardless of the general approach you use, here are some specific techniques tutors can use to help writers with proofreading:

- *Explain how you find errors.* In other words, do your best to think out loud to help the writer learn from your example.
- *Explain suggestions according to the writer's intended meaning.* ("With the commas, it sounds like you mean. . . ." or "When you change tenses, I can't tell if you mean. . . .").

    Also, remember that rules are made to be broken and what the writer is doing may be creative and effective even if he doesn't fully understand it. Be open to this, and talk with the writer about whether or not it works. If you are both unsure, seek another opinion.

- *Compare specific strong and weak examples from the paper.* ("You use passive voice in this sentence, but over here, you use active voice. See how this sentence is less wordy?")

- *Let the writer try out strategies on his own.* ("Ok, I've shown you how to change this sentence to remove the dangling modifier. How would you fix this next dangling modifier?")

- *Maintain a healthy sense of doubt.* ("This might be wrong—I tend to get mixed up about lie/lay. Have you brought your handbook?") A tutor isn't expected to be The Grammar God. Tutors are expected to help writers learn to help themselves. Modeling use of a handbook is a great way to do that. Maintain doubt also by asking gently, "Why did you do this?" The answer may reveal that the writer is laboring under a misconception—or, it may reveal that you have misunderstood his intention.

At the end of this chapter (see Appendix A), you will find a list of techniques writers and tutors can use to check quickly for ideas and organization before embarking on proofreading (also see Trupe, this volume, for more on organization). You will also find a list of proofreading techniques to use in locating surface features (see Appendix B), a table that tries to match techniques with writing problems (see Appendix C), and suggested guidelines for prioritizing errors (see Appendix D). Use them as a guide for reflecting on various approaches to helping writers with their proofreading.

Complicating Matters

So it's as easy as that? Well, it's probably not that easy. In practice, these strategies have mixed results. Here are some of the difficulties we've run into in the writing center where I work. How would you address them?

Writers may regard the writing center as a place to share the burden. They may feel resentment and think, "I don't know this stuff. I did all I can do and now I've come here for help, not to be told to do it myself. If I could do it myself, I wouldn't need to come here." Given the great amount of time some writers invest in ideas, research, and revising, isn't it fair for them to ask the writing center to proofread for them so that they can devote more of their time to ideas, research, and revision?

Many writing centers have embraced the goal of empowering *student writers* to become *writers,* which involves, in part, helping students to learn the practices and habits of writers with *real-world* audiences and goals. Yet in workplace and other so-called real world settings, writers often turn to someone else for help with proofreading, because outside readers are more effective proofreaders. In fact, research by Glynda Hull (1987) examined just this point. Hull asked groups of more-skilled and less-skilled college writers to proofread several essays, some of which were written by others, some of which were written by the the writers in the study. Hull found that more-skilled writers were better than less-skilled writers at proofreading papers written by someone else. But the two groups performed about the same when proofreading their own work—neither group corrected many errors at all. If proofreading is best done by someone other than the writer, should a writing center offer to proofread for writers, rather than helping writers learn how to proofread for themselves?

Writers may not know enough to share the burden. Some writers may honestly not be able to find errors themselves. For example, ESL writers who come to the writing center for help with articles and prepositions are often unable to locate problems with these words (see Ritter, this volume). Even when we try our best to explain the rules, ESL writers may not be able to spot problems with articles. This is because many languages do not have articles (those that do often use them differently from English), and because the rules for article use in English are surprisingly complex. One ESL speaker, a Japanese-born college professor, noted, "I have studied articles for 17 years, and I am finally beginning to feel I've mastered them."[3] As this professor knew, ESL writers need practice and experience to acquire a good sense of articles. Thirty minutes, even with careful explanation, isn't likely to make a big difference. How can a tutor know how much progress is realistic to expect in a proofreading session?

Some errors may be normal side effect of writing improvement. As writers experiment with new techniques, it stands to reason that they will make mistakes while they are learning to master those techniques. To test this theory, Richard H. Haswell compared the errors made by college freshmen, sophomores, juniors, and post-college employees. He found that college students' writing did improve, and that they continued to make mistakes at the same rate while they were improving, but the mistakes were allied to the improvement. For example, as college students learned to write more complex sentences, they would make new mistakes which could not be made in simpler sentences. One implication of Haswell's finding is that undue effort to prevent the mistakes may also hinder the improvement. Given this, how much effort should a tutor spend on helping writers correct mistakes?

A student had worked diligently on a paper with one of the tutors in our writing center, only to return after she had received a C grade. At the bottom of her paper, the instructor wrote, "Next time, proofread!" Though the student did not try to blame the tutor, she was clearly discouraged. And the tutor felt terrible because he had not recognized several major errors in the paper. What would you say to this tutor? What should the tutor say to the student?

Further Reading

Bishop, Wendy, ed. 1997. *Elements of Alternate Style*. Portsmouth, NH: Boynton/Cook.

If ever a book made the point that rules of grammar and proper usage were made to be broken, this is it. Various authors contribute chapters to this book covering such topics as fractured narratives, risk taking, radical revision, and alternative grammars. This is a delightful read for anyone who has thought about breaking conventions creatively, and a must for anyone in danger of becoming too serious about correctness.

Hartwell, Patrick. 1985. Grammar, Grammars, and the Teaching of Grammar. *College English* 47: 105–27.

In all that has been written about grammar and the teaching of writing, this article is a stand out for the clarity with which it frames the debate. Hartwell explains the various meanings of grammar and why matters of usage, correctness, and style are fundamentally different from linguistics and the language we all acquire as we grow up. This article also helps in understanding why research findings have shown that grammar instruction in school does not tend to improve writing.

Hunter, Susan, and Ray Wallace, eds. 1995. *The Place of Grammar in Writing Instruction.* Portsmouth, NH: Boynton/Cook.

This book of essays offers a current and historical perspective on the debate about grammar and writing, focusing especially on the college level. Many of the essays challenge the idea that grammar instruction has no place in teaching writing, and some offer ideas for how to incorporate grammar instruction in ways that students will find lively and interesting. The contributing authors include college composition teachers and writing center directors.

Notes

1. This chapter began as a presentation at the National Conference on Peer Tutoring in Writing, Plattsburgh State University of New York, November 6–8, 1998.

2. David Bartholomae, "The Study of Error," *College Composition and Communication* 31 (October 1980), 253–69.

3. *English Composition for Non-Native Speakers.* Videotape. (Miami: University of Miami, 1996).

Works Cited

Bartholomae, D. 1980. "The Study of Error." *College Composition and Communication* 31: 253–69.

Cazort, D. 1997. *Under the Grammar Hammer: The 25 Most Important Grammar Mistakes and How to Avoid Them.* Los Angeles: Lowell House.

Clark, I. L. 1998. *Writing in the Center,* 3rd ed. Dubuque, IA: Kendall/Hunt.

Connors, R. J., and Lunsford, A. A. 1988. "Frequency of Formal Errors in Current College Writing, or Ma & Pa Kettle Do Research." *College Composition and Communication* 39: 395–409.

English Composition for Non-Native Speakers. 1996. Videotape. Miami: University of Miami.

Hairston, M. 1981. "Not All Errors Are Created Equal: Nonacademic Readers in the Professions Respond to Lapses in Usage." *College English* 41: 794–806.

Haswell, R. H. 1988. "Error and Change in Student Writing." *Written Communication* 5: 479–99.

Hull, G. 1985. "Research on Error and Correction." In *Perspectives on Research and Scholarship in Composition,* ed. B. McClelland and T. Donovan, 162–84. New York: Modern Language Association.

North, S. 1984. "The Idea of a Writing Center." *College English* 46 (5): 433–46.

Shaughnessy, M. 1977. *Errors and Expectations.* New York: Oxford.

Williams, J. 1981. "The Phenomenology of Error." *College Composition and Communication* 32: 152–68.

Appendix A

Global Techniques Writers
and Tutors Can Use for Ideas and Organization

Before beginning to proofread for surface errors, look carefully at ideas and organization.

- ### *Underline the thesis.*

Is there a thesis? Where is it? Does it accurately reflect the paper? Is it interesting, or is it a just-add-water, 3-part boring thesis? If the writer agrees the ideas are weak, help the writer make a plan to contact the instructor and ask for an extension to start over.

- ### *Help the writer create a descriptive outline for the paper.*

What does each paragraph or section do? What does the paper as a whole do? It is one thing to know *what a paragraph says,* but just as important to know *what it does* to strengthen the paper.

- ### *Underline transitions between paragraphs.*

Are there enough transitions? Do the transitions help to connect the paragraphs to the thesis? Do the transitions show how different paragraphs relate to each other, or do they just mark items in a list ("One thing . . . and another thing . . . and another thing . . .")?

- ### *Work with the writer to create an abstract of the paper.*

Start with the thesis and condense each paragraph to one sentence. If this proves to be too difficult to do, you may have located a problem with paragraph coherence. Fit all of this into one paragraph. Is it clear how each idea leads to the next? Is the abstract coherent? If not, revise the abstract. Next, using the abstract as a guide, revise the paper.

- *Underline each important idea in a different color. Then underline information related to each idea in the same color.*

Is supporting material located near the idea it is supposed to support? Can you see a pattern in the arrangement of this information, or is everything mixed together?

- *Examine suspect paragraphs (unusually long, unusually short, can't tell what it does in a descriptive outline, can't condense to a sentence, etc.) by assigning a level of generality to each sentence.*

Too many level-one sentences? No level-one sentences? Enough level-two and -three sentences to support each level-one?

- *Underline the new or important information in each sentence.*

Is this information located near stress points? We usually stress the words before or after a pause, especially at the end of the sentence. It-clefts ("It is interesting to . . ."), that-clefts ("That a problem arose is . . .") and there transformations ("There is a consensus . . .") can create additional stress points. Does information already provided or a transitional cue ("By contrast," "What is more," "Despite this fact," etc.) prepare readers for new information?

Appendix B

Proofreading Techniques Writers
and Tutors Can Use for Surface Features

Get a Fresh Perspective

- Take a break (as little as 5 minutes) between writing and proofreading.
- Ask someone to read the paper to you, or read the paper to someone else.
- Read the paper into a tape recorder; play back the tape while you follow along.
- Listen for:

    1. Places where what is read differs from what is written,
    2. Places where the reader stumbles for any reason, and
    3. Places where the listener gets distracted, confused, or bored.

Slow Down

- Cover the writing with a ruler or piece of paper so you can see only one line of text at a time.
- Read backward, sentence by sentence (for unclear sentence structure, redundancy).
- Read backward, word by word (for typos and spelling mistakes).
- Circle verbs (to locate passive voice, strong verbs, tense shifts).
- Circle prepositional phrases (to locate wordiness).
- Point at punctuation marks as you name each piece of a citation (for proper citation format; for example, "Last name comma year. Date colon page numbers.")

Personalize the Process

- Help the writer to begin an editing checklist of frequent mistakes. Keep the checklist for use with subsequent papers. Update it every time a paper is returned.

- Read through the paper several times, looking for a different problem each time.

Use a Computer

- Print a draft designed especially for proofreading.

- Doublespace. Put in extra hard returns so that each sentence starts on a new line (to locate fragments).

- Use 14-point or larger type (for apostrophe and comma problems).

- Use the find/replace function for items on your editing checklist, including wordiness flags ("to be" verbs, prepositions, etc.) and typos (from/form, extra spaces after periods, unnecessary commas, etc.).

- Use spell-check and grammar-check software. These programs are hardly foolproof, but when interpreted with a tutor who is a good editor, they can be helpful.

- Tell the writer about good online grammar Web sites and telephone hotlines. These can usually be found by visiting writing center home pages on the Internet.

Proofreading Techniques

These proofreading techniques (below) can help you locate different kinds of problems (right).	Spelling	Wrong Word	Incorrect Citation Format	Verb Tense Problems	Subj.-Verb Agreement	Pronoun Agreement	Misplaced Modifiers
Take a break before proofreading.	X	X	X	X	X	X	X
Print a proofreading draft with extra space in margins and between sentences.	X	X	X	X	X	X	X
Create a personalized editing checklist based on your previous writing.	X	X	X	X	X	X	X
Read paper more than once, looking for different problems each time.	X	X	X	X	X	X	X
Read aloud to someone else.		X		X	X	X	X
Have someone read aloud while you follow along.	X	X		X	X		X
Physically cover up all but the line you're reading.	X	X	X				
Read backwards, word by word.	X						
Read backwards, sentence by sentence.	X	X	X	X	X	X	X
Point at words as you read them aloud to yourself.	X	X					
Circle all verbs, then check for tense, agreement, voice, mood, etc.				X	X		X
Circle prepositions, then check for clarity. If possible, reword to eliminate prepositions.							X
Circle commas, then check to see if they are correctly used.							X
Point at and name punctuation as you read.		X					X
Use find/replace function to search for likely misspellings or wrong words (e.g., their/there).	X	X					
Use spell check software. (Warning: This software won't catch all errors.)	X						
Use grammar check software. (Warning: This software won't catch all errors and is frequently incorrect.)	X	X		X	X		

(*continued on page 124*)

Proofreading Techniques *(continued from page 123)*

These proofreading techniques (below) can help you locate different kinds of problems (right).	Sentence Fragments	Comma Splices	General Punctuation Problems	Wordiness
Take a break before proofreading.	X	X	X	X
Print a proofreading draft with extra space in margins and between sentences.	X	X	X	X
Create a personalized editing checklist based on your previous writing.	X	X	X	X
Read paper more than once, looking for different problems each time.	X	X	X	X
Read aloud to someone else.				X
Have someone read aloud while you follow along.	X	X	X	X
Physically cover up all but the line you're reading.			X	
Read backwards, word by word.				
Read backwards, sentence by sentence.	X	X	X	
Point at words as you read them aloud to yourself.				
Circle all verbs, then check for tense, agreement, voice, mood, etc.	X	X		
Circle prepositions, then check for clarity. If possible, reword to eliminate prepositions				X
Circle commas, then check to see if they are correctly used.	X	X	X	
Point at and name punctuation as you read.	X	X	X	
Use find/replace function to search for likely misspellings or wrong words (e.g., their/there).				
Use spell check software. (Warning: This software won't catch all errors.)				
Use grammar check software. (Warning: This software won't catch all errors and is frequently incorrect.)	X	X	X	X

Linear Coherence ("Flow")	Paragraph Structure	Support of Ideas	Overall Organization	Thesis
X	X	X	X	X
X	X	X	X	X
X	X	X	X	X
X	X	X	X	X
X		X	X	X
X		X	X	X

Appendix D

Error Priority Guidelines

Remember, you'll need to read the entire paper before you can prioritize errors. Try to focus on errors in this order:

1. Errors which affect comprehension of the text
2. Errors which the writer is especially concerned about
3. Frequent occurrences of the same error
4. Errors which can be fixed by learning a rule
5. Errors which don't violate a particular rule, but rather are matters of idiom or preference

When several different errors fall into the same category, you and the writer should decide which errors to address first. Here are some points to consider as you decide:

- Which errors is the writer interested in or ready to address?
- Which errors are likely to bother readers the most? (You might want to refer to Douglas Cazort's list of "Five Uncommonly Serious Mistakes" in *Under the Grammar Hammer. You might also ask which errors the teacher has complained about in the past.*)
- Which errors are most likely to recur in future papers?
- Which errors do you feel the most comfortable explaining?

14

Using Others' Words

Quoting, Summarizing, and Documenting Sources

Mary Mortimore Dossin

Many colleges and universities publish plagiarism policies that are harsh and punitive. Words like "theft," "integrity," and "character issue" give the issue a moral dimension that calls into question the ethics of individuals who plagiarize. What tutors are more likely to encounter in the writing center, however, are not intentional plagiarists but students who are genuinely befuddled by what Libby Miles terms "the contradictions of American academic writing":

> Show you have done your research *but* write something new and original.
> Appeal to experts and authorities *but* improve upon or disagree with them.
> Improve your English by mimicking what you hear and read *but*
>   use your own words, your own voice.
> Give credit where credit is due *but* make your own significant contribution.[1]

Not an easy course to navigate! Tutors can help.

Some Background

Definitions of plagiarism vary according to time, place, and discipline. The concepts of authorship[2] and originality[3] are attributed to the eighteenth century in Western cultures. Libby Miles writes that other cultures are much less insistent upon careful documenting of sources than American institutions,[4] and Irene L. Clark notes that imitation has had an important role in learning in certain times and cultures.[5] In fact, in Chinese culture, copying classic authors is actually seen as a virtue, a way of honoring those traditional authors, according to Kristen Walker in the *Writing Lab Newsletter*.[6] In addition, Walker found in her work with engineering students—for whom English is a second

---

SEE DISCUSSION TOPIC **#2** AT THE END OF THIS BOOK

language—that disciplines also vary in their definitions of plagiarism.[7] (See Ritter, this volume.)

Here and now, however, and in most disciplines, plagiarism is a serious issue that has recently acquired a new twist: the Internet. Students now have abundant opportunities to lift "prewritten" term papers off of Web pages like those on the Web site Genius Papers, which offers students "unlimited access into our database of hundreds upon hundreds of papers" for $9.95 per year. As well, professors can now subscribe to Internet services like those of Plagiarism.org to detect papers pillaged by their students. The jury is still out on whether the bad guys or the sheriffs will win on this one. In any case, intentional plagiarists are not as frequent in the writing center as are genuinely confused students who want to avoid something about which their professor has given them dire warnings; when viewed in this way, there really are no bad guys and sheriffs.

What to Do

An occasional scene in most writing centers is a student sitting at a computer surrounded by photocopied articles with highlighted passages. She picks up one of the articles, leafs through it, then sets it in front of her and writes a bit on the computer. Then she picks up another and repeats the process. It's slow going. By the time she approaches me or one of the peer writing tutors to ask about documentation guidelines, it's almost too late. Her chance of producing an honest, original paper has been seriously jeopardized.

Inexperienced researchers, or those who have developed bad habits like those above, need clarification of the skills demanded by a research paper assignment: gathering information, analyzing and synthesizing the information, and communicating one's own understanding of this information to others. Learning that such skills are essential in the working world can help instill in students the motivation needed to master them. Writing centers need to be proactive rather than just reactive on the issues of research papers. Workshops and class visits can get out the message about the kind of early work that is necessary for an original paper.

Students need to know that they can come to the writing center for assistance long before they are ready to write a draft of the paper. Plagiarism begins much earlier: when the topic is chosen, when notes are taken (or not taken), and when the analysis and synthesis stage is done (or not done). Writing tutors can be most effective in helping students to avoid plagiarism if they intervene at these early stages.

The first real necessity is a topic the writer cares about. Writing an honest paper is hard work, and students are unlikely to be motivated to invest the energy and curiosity needed unless they have chosen a topic that is truly a question they need to answer for themselves. Talking with a tutor or the professor at this stage can help the writer discover a topic and an angle to which he can commit himself.

Then, in order to use the words of others effectively and appropriately, the writer must both master his sources and break his connection to their language and structure. There are two necessities for doing these things: taking honest notes and building a structure and language that evolve from the writer's own analysis and synthesis of the information being gathered. Student writers often don't know these requirements or don't have the skills available to follow them effectively. Tutors need to be prepared to help students during these stages in the process.

For the first, copying information directly from sources or highlighting it on a photocopy without taking time to make sense of the information in one's own language will lead to a plagiarized paper no matter how diligent one is about the fine points of documentation style. Honest notes—particularly if they are on note cards—with direct quotations clearly noted and most of the information in the writer's own words will make the writing of an original paper much more likely. The skills of paraphrasing and summarizing are essential for honest notes. Invaluable and detailed material on these skills (and all other aspects of writing research papers) can be found in Diana Hacker's *A Writer's Reference* and on the Purdue Online Writing Lab (OWL). The Purdue OWL,[8] for example, has detailed instructions on "Quoting, Paraphrasing, and Summarizing" that first compares and contrasts the terms, then gives an example illustrating their use, and finally offers a sample essay on which to practice these skills. An exercise entitled "Paraphrasing" gives some sample passages on which a writer can practice. In another handout, sample answers to this exercise are given, which a writer can compare to her own work. Tutor assistance with such an exercise would be helpful to those writers for whom the written information is not enough. Doing such work directly with a writer's own sources can also be very useful.

Analysis and synthesis of material is also essential. This stage is often skipped because students don't know it's necessary, haven't allowed time for it, or don't know how to do it. Tutors can help by using the Twenty Questions for Research Writing handout at the end of this chapter to enable a writer to talk or write her way through this important step. Daily writing—what Peter Elbow terms "making a mess" in *On Writing*—will help more than anything else. The writer should answer the questions, whether verbally or in writing, in her own language. Set the source aside while the questions are being answered. When this is done, both the language and the structure that evolve as the writer answers the questions will be the writer's own. This work is most beneficial if it is spread out over the several weeks in which the writer is researching her subject. Returning to questions at different stages is useful.

A live body—the tutor—is of enormous benefit at this stage. Nothing beats the presence of another when a writer is wrestling with ideas and striving for new insight. The best gift a tutor can give a writer at this stage is her or his real curiosity about the topic. Talking writers through this stage will not work if it is a regimented process. Tutors need energy and curiosity as much as writers do. Tutors who are eager to learn more about a wide variety of subjects will be good at this. Their questions will arise naturally out of their own enthusiasm of discovery. Tutors who are just going through the motions will confirm the writer's suspicions that research papers are a tedious and boring exercise in demonstrating command of the conventions of grammar and format.

After honest notes and an original structure have been achieved, the writer is ready to learn about techniques for weaving the words and ideas of others into her own text. The two most common mistakes of unintentional plagiarists are failing to cite paraphrased material and failing to put language from the source into quotation marks. Here, too, tutors can help by pointing out useful written material that clearly illustrates ways of using the others' words and ideas appropriately. Once again, reach for Hacker. In her section on research writing the author includes principles and examples on integrating information from sources. Sections on using signal phrases give helpful examples. There are also rules and examples on using ellipsis marks and brackets and setting off long quotations. Such a source should be available in the writing center and tutors should be skilled in using it. The Purdue Online Writing Lab is also an invaluable source on all aspects of writing honestly. Both Hacker and the Purdue OWL have helpful information on documentation styles for MLA and APA that is much more accessible than official manuals. The Purdue OWL handouts can be printed out and taken home by the writer for further work and assistance.

Complicating Matters

All of the above assumes a situation in which writers have some sense of the early work to be done and know that they can come in to the writing center for help with skills they're unsure of. Often, however, this is not the case. We've all seen frantic writers who come into the writing center with a paper that's due tomorrow. Help with introducing material from sources and documenting it properly is still possible of course. But what about the "patchwork quilt" papers that barely stitch together information lifted almost intact from sources? Options are limited, and it's possible none of them will be successful.

The writer needs to be asked about material that seems to be copied from sources. This can be done gently and politely—"Are these your words?"—but tutors need to communicate clearly that the consequences of plagiarism can be dire. Tutors should know the plagiarism policies of their own institutions so that they can be specific and not just hand out vague threats. I recommend that tutors urge the writer to check with the instructor or, if that's not possible, to get a second opinion from another tutor whenever there is a question about how the writer is using sources.

Students tend to have two responses to such advice. One is that the writer will simply leave—maybe not immediately but relatively soon. The writer hasn't received what she or he wants, so help will be sought elsewhere. Tutors should not consider this a failure on their part. The message has been given and received. Perhaps the writer will know better in the future. And if not, an essential lesson in tutoring as in life is that we have little control over the behavior of others.

A second, more positive possibility is that the writer will be eager or at least willing to work with the material for what it is: a work-in-progress. In truth this is what we often if not always see in the writing center, an early draft, ripe for revision. Writers don't always realize this initially, of course, and some aren't glad to hear it. But others will be. When this happens, the draft becomes a discovery draft with which to work, and the Twenty Questions that follow (see Figure 14–1) can be very useful.

Figure 14–1. Twenty Questions for Research Writing

Research writing can be described as follows:
Gathering information ↔ Analyzing and synthesizing ↔ Communicating/ writing
Daily writing will help you with a research paper more than anything else: Every day, take ten or fifteen minutes to answer one of the questions.

1. What topic have you chosen for your research and why?
2. What do you know now about the topic?
3. What do you want to find out?
4. Are you aware of any controversies regarding this topic? If so, what are they, and what is your current stand on the issue?
5. Have you noticed any areas of disagreement among your sources?
6. Which of the viewpoints seems the most valid to you? Why?
7. Do you have any unanswered questions at this point?
8. Did anything surprise you as you gathered information?
9. What has been the most interesting aspect of the material you've gathered so far?
10. After reviewing your data or sources, what do you see as the latest problems in the field of your topic?
11. What do you think are the important facts of the matter?
12. Are there better ways of interpreting the reported information that previous authors have ignored?
13. How can you relate these previous studies into a general picture?
14. What new insight can you contribute?
15. Considering all of the above, how would you sum up your current attitude toward your topic in a sentence or two?
16. If you decide to use the answer to Question 15 as a working thesis for your paper, what information will you have to give your readers to

(*continued on page 133*)

convince them that your stand is a valid one? What questions of theirs will you have to answer? (The answers to these questions will suggest major points for your outline.)

17. What one real question will your paper answer?
18. What is your current answer to this question?
19. What information do you have to support this?
20. What information do you still need to gather?

Not all of these questions will work for all topics, of course, so use them to deal with whatever information and topics have been chosen. Go back to questions at different points in the process and see how their answers change as more information is gathered and the topic is re-examined.

Set the draft aside so that the writer can break his strong connection to the language and structure of the source. Then work through the Twenty Questions, perhaps not all but those that seem useful. This will give the writer a chance to construct a framework on which to build an original paper. A similar approach is a variation of Peter Elbow's idea of the Instant Version.[9] The writer again sets aside all sources, notes, and drafts and simply writes a quick version of the paper, giving him a place to start. The results would have been better if these had been done earlier, of course, but this is an imperfect world and none of us always does what we should. We can still learn—and perhaps do better next time. The writing center maxim that we are not about better papers but better writers applies here.

Ultimately, it pays to remember that writing a good research paper takes practice. It's something like directing a chorus. Once the writer has found the sources, he must then give each of them a role or a voice in the chorus of different voices that will become his research paper. He can allow some to keep their own voices (direct quotes), but most of them must be blended with his own (paraphrases and summaries) to make the paper author-itative. When viewed in this way, we gain greater appreciation for what goes into a good research paper and a better understanding of how tutors can help.

Further Reading

Bowers, Neal. 1997. *Words for the Taking: The Hunt for a Plagiarist.* New York: Norton.

A fascinating account of a poet's search for the person plagiarizing his work, it gives fine insight into the state of mind of the one who is being plagiarized.

Moody, Pam. 1993. "Tutors' Column: A Slight Case of Plagiarism." *Writing Lab Newsletter* 17 (5): 9–11.

A tutor writes about the sense of betrayal and failure she experiences when a student with whom she is working plagiarizes a paper.

"Plagiarism in the Classroom: Readers Explain How They Define It and How They Deal with It." 1994. *The Council Chronicle* 3 (5): 14–15.

This is one way tutors can see the diversity of instructors' views and approaches to plagiarism, and a reminder that not all teachers see the matter in the same way. After reading this article, writing center tutors might consider how their own faculty differ on the question of plagiarism. (*The Council Chronicle* is a newsletter published by the National Council of Teachers of English in Urbana, Illinois.)

The Internet makes available innumerable plagiarism policies of colleges and universities. They make an interesting study of differences in approach, tone, and policy.

Notes

1. Libby Miles, *Avoiding Plagiarism* (Handout from Purdue University Writing Lab, 1997).

2. Lisa Ede, "The Concept of Authorship: An Historical Perspective" (ERIC Document No. ED266481).

3. Thomas Mallon, *Stolen Words: Forays into the Origins and Ravages of Plagiarism* (NY: Ticknor & Fields, 1989), 24.

4. Miles.

5. Irene Lurkis Clark, "Collaboration and Ethics in Writing Center Pedagogy," *Writing Center Journal* 9 (1) (1988): 8.

6. Kristen Walker, "Consulting with ESL Students in an Engineering Writing Center: Issues and Strategies for Dealing with the Problem of Plagiarism," *Writing Lab Newsletter* 21 (6) (1997): 3.

7. Walker, 2.

8. The Purdue OWL may be found at <http://owl.english.purdue.edu/>

9. Peter Elbow, *Writing with Power* (NY: Oxford Univ. Press, 1981), 64–5.

Works Cited

Clark, I. L. 1988. "Collaboration and Ethics in Writing Center Pedagogy." *The Writing Center Journal* 9 (1): 3–12.

Ede, L. Nov. 1985. "The Concept of Authorship: An Historical Perspective." Speech/Conference Paper. ERIC Document No.: ED266481.

Elbow, P. 1981. *Writing with Power.* NY: Oxford University Press.

Genius Papers. 10 Jan. 1999. 19 May 1999 <http://geniuspapers.com/>

Hacker, D. 1999. *A Writer's Reference,* 4th ed. Boston: Bedford/St. Martin's.

Mallon, T. 1989. *Stolen Words: Forays into the Origins and Ravages of Plagiarism.* NY: Ticknor & Fields.

Miles, L. 1997. *Avoiding Plagiarism.* Handout from Purdue University Writing Lab.

Peter Elbow on Writing. 1995. Videocassette. Media Education Foundation.

Plagiarism.org. 1999. iParadigms, Inc. 19 May 1999. <http://plagiarism.org/>

Purdue Online Writing Lab. 1999. Purdue University Writing Lab. 19 May 1999 <http://owl.english.purdue.edu:>

Walker, K. 1997. "Consulting with ESL Students in an Engineering Writing Center: Issues and Strategies for Dealing with the Problem of Plagiarism." *Writing Lab Newsletter* 21 (6): 1–5.

15

Becoming a Resource

Multiple Ways of Thinking About
Information and the Writing Conference

Sandra J. Eckard and Jennifer E. Staben

Our purpose in this chapter is not to provide a definitive list of resources. Tutoring is not about finding a resource—print or cyber—and bringing it with you to the conferencing table. It is about becoming a resource. To become a resource, we believe, tutors need to think not only about what kinds of information to use, but more importantly, when, how, and with whom.

> It is 3:00 P.M. on a Thursday afternoon and you are working with Lu, an international student from China. The seven typed pages that she has spent days researching and writing sit on the table between you, and she is reading from the first page. It is clear as you scan the paper before you and listen to her words that Lu is having trouble at several levels. Though her topic, "Violence and Children," is interesting, her main points don't seem connected to one another and her sentences often wrap around themselves—sliding from clarity to confusion. As you are making mental notes to yourself about her paper, Lu suddenly stops reading in midsentence and asks, "I have some questions about citing from the Internet. Will you show me how to do that, too?"

The many layers of advice and assistance that Lu requires in this scenario suggest the complexity inherent in any tutoring session; a tutor must draw on a wide range of resources to address both Lu's immediate concerns about documentation and her long-term needs involving organization and ESL writing. Some of these resources are internal; every tutor possesses knowledge and skills that they have gained from their experiences as a student, writer, and tutor. However, tutors may also need to turn to external sources of information

SEE DISCUSSION TOPICS #2 AND #5 AT THE END OF THIS BOOK

to help writers—sources such as grammar handbooks, style manuals, hand-outs, Web pages, books, journal articles, and newsletters. Though the need for additional resources usually arises within a specific conference with a particular student, not all of these resources can actually be used during a tutoring session. Some materials contribute to the ongoing development of you as a tutor or of your tutee as a writer. With this in mind, we have designed the discussion that follows not only to suggest some types of resources you might look for, but to help you see that becoming a resource means more than simply knowing where to find information.

During the Tutoring Session

Handbooks, style manuals, and dictionaries are the materials most tutors think of as resources. A writer asks you a question about commas or works cited pages and you turn to texts like these because the issue seems complicated or you are unsure of the answer. However, before you next take a book off the shelf, consider that consulting a resource is a teachable moment for the writer: what they learn depends largely on what you do. What does a writer learn if you grab a handbook, flip it open to page 47, and simply announce the answer? What does a writer learn if you hand her the *Publication Manual of the American Psychological Association* and tell her that all she needs to know about the Reference page is right there? Decisions about what to do with a resource begin with the writers themselves. How can you help them be empowered rather than overpowered by a handbook or style guide?

Modeling and Facilitating

Somewhere along the continuum between total control and complete hands-off lie two approaches, modeling and facilitating, that can help you both to locate answers to questions and develop as writers and independent learners. Modeling your own methods for consulting a resource—whether searching for alternatives to the word "use" in a thesaurus or looking through the *MLA Handbook* for how to cite Web pages—is just one of many ways to demonstrate "experienced writer" behavior. In these cases, modeling involves walking your tutee through both the physical and intellectual processes you go through when searching for information. For example, my tutee wants to know if she should spell out the numbers in her paper, so I show her how I would find out that information in the handbook she owns, *The Everyday Writer* (Lunsford and Connors). I position the text between us so she can see what I'm doing and I talk her through my decision to use the "Quick Access Menu" in the front and my methods for locating and interpreting the information I find. The value of both showing and telling your tutee what you are doing to find the answer is that they will not only learn the information but how to access it later on their own if they need to (see Macauley, this volume).

You might also consider giving your tutee more control of the learning process by shifting from the role of model to facilitator. To become an effective user of resources, writers need to do more than observe; they need to try out search procedures, get a feel for them, and learn from their own mistakes. These can be especially fruitful activities under the eye of someone more experienced—someone like a tutor who can offer explanations, suggestions, and encouragement. To act as a facilitator, you must hand the text over to the writer and let him initiate the process; your responsibility is to coach from the sidelines.

One concern tutors may have about these two practices—especially facilitating—is time. Because time runs by so quickly, it may seem simpler and more efficient for you to provide the writer with the needed information. This can be especially tempting if the information is easy or difficult to locate or if you can answer the question without consulting a source. But what has been lost by doing all the work for the student? At the same time, acting as a facilitator is not always the best option. The decision about when to put the resource directly into the writer's hands should be based on your sense of the writer and their situation at that moment—whether you have been working with them for only twenty minutes or over the course of an entire semester. Are they totally overwhelmed and one step away from a nervous breakdown? Is their paper due in five hours? Then, think about modeling. If not, consider taking a step back and giving them more control.

Thinking Beyond the Bookshelf

Are handbooks, style guides, and other reference texts the only useful resources you can use during a tutoring session? Once you start exploring the possibilities for how to incorporate outside materials into your tutoring sessions, also consider pushing the boundaries of what types of resources you might use. The approaches of modeling and facilitating can make teachable moments out of basic questions on mechanics and form. Imagine what they can do for a more complex process like finding information for a research paper. Let's say your writer has been asked to write a paper on the conflict in Northern Ireland and he must use a variety of sources. If your writing center has Internet access, you can use part of your tutoring session to introduce him to Web sites like My Virtual Reference Desk <http://www.refdesk.com> or the Internet Public Library <http://www.ipc.org>. If your institution's library has an online presence, you can help him track down print sources without leaving the writing center. Facilitating is an especially useful practice to use when helping writers explore resources on the Internet. If your tutee physically types in the information and makes choices, she will be much more likely to remember the procedures. As a facilitator, you can use questions to prompt, explanations to clarify, and suggestions to help the writer when she gets stuck.

Whatever approach you choose or resource you decide to explore, the learning does not stop when the information is located. The difficulty with many handbooks and style manuals is that their content is often clear to a writer who is already familiar with the rules they describe, but less coherent to one who is not. Similarly, finding resources is only one step in the longer process of writing a research paper. Your writer finds the page on comma splices, but throws up her hands at the dense text and endless list of examples. How might you help her make the connection between the rules on the page and her own writing? Or, the writer you are working with has found numerous sources—print and cyber—on his topic, but is not sure how to integrate the information with her own thoughts and ideas. How might you help her? Instead of thinking of resources as the end to a conversation, think of them as the beginning of a longer discussion—one that might involve lots of examples and scratch paper.

Follow-up for the Writer

"Our goal is not to make better papers, but to make better writers." This is posted on many a writing center bulletin board, but what happens when deadlines and schedules get in the way? What if follow-up sessions or regular meetings are just not possible? Are there other ways that you can help a writer work on the long-term skills they need? Yes! There are lots of materials in print and on the Web that can help a writer develop independently. For example, consider recommending a student-friendly text like *The Right Handbook* (Belanoff et al.) to a tutee. Though not a substitute for one-to-one interaction, this handbook bypasses the usual confusing lists of rules for a wider and more readable discussion of the general conventions of academic writing. It covers everything from language myths to punctuation; practice activities are included along with playful comments about what it means to think about writing.

In addition, the Internet is a constantly changing resource with many jumping off points for writers. Dave's ESL Cafe <http://www.eslcafe.com> is a wonderful Web site for ESL writers; it contains everything from definitions of slang and idioms to grammar quizzes to e-mail discussion groups. As well as providing information for ESL writers, Purdue's Online Writing Lab <http://owl.english.purdue.edu> also maintains links to general writing resources and to other online writer centers. Writers visiting this site can access over 130 instructional handouts. If you think your writer could use some support as they work through an essay, consider sending her to the Writer's Web <http://www.urich.edu/~writing/wweb.html>. This is a site that offers useful and readable information about every stage of the writing process. Finally, native and non-native speakers alike can benefit from the LinguaCenter's Grammar Safari <http://deil.lang.uiuc.edu/web.pages/grammarsafari.html>, an interactive site that sends writers on a hunt through the Internet to "bag" examples of specific grammar structures. Though the selections we've mentioned provide writers with a chance to take charge of their own learning, they can also create excellent opportunities for dialogue between a student and writer after an initial conference.

Follow-up for the Tutor

What does it mean to be a tutor? What kinds of information do you need to know to be a successful tutor? How does your own writing process influence how you talk with writers about the act of composing? Since the 1970s, tutors and writing center staffers have been talking with each other. Joining this conversation can help you learn about writing and tutoring.

The Writing Lab Newsletter and *The Writing Center Journal* are the two primary journals of the profession. There are also many online sources, with the National Writing Centers Association Web page <http://departments. colgate.edu /diw/nwcaowls.html> being a great place to follow up on your interests. The National Conference on Peer Tutoring in Writing is an excellent place to meet other tutors. Each year more than 350 tutors from around the country attend the conference (usually held in the East or Midwest) to talk about their writing centers, get new ideas, and just have fun. More information about the NCPTW may be found at <http://www.chss.iup.edu /wc /ncptw>.

Looking for something in particular? An excellent resource you can have on your shelves is Murphy, Law, and Sherwood's *Writing Centers: An Annotated Bibliography* because it organizes many writing center publications, even those not included in *The Writing Lab Newsletter* and *The Writing Center Journal.* Although it is now becoming dated, it is a wonderful starting point for seeing where, when, and how others have entered and shaped conversations about topics you would like to investigate.

In the three sections that follow, we explore aspects of tutoring where using outside resources can be helpful, and we recommend some resources that you can use to enter the conversation including the most valuable resource you can bring to any tutoring table: yourself.

Knowledge About Language

"Because it sounds right." As experienced writers, there is so much we do—so many choices we make—as we compose and revise simply because our ear tells us one way sounds better than another. We decide to use "slept" instead of "had slept" in a sentence or we change "These materials are needed by students" to "Students need these materials" in the middle of a paragraph because it just feels like a better thing to do. However, this instinct alone is not enough for a tutor to help inexperienced or non-native writers make informed choices in their own writing.

So, how do you move beyond fuzzy statements to concrete and detailed explanations that will help a writer understand their decisions about language? One way is to consult resources that make the rules and structures behind language choices conscious and available to you. Though they are not places to send tutees nor are they quick-fix solutions to your grammar questions, books like *A Student's Grammar of the English Language* (Greenbaum and Quirk) or *Doing Grammar* (Morenberg) are detailed texts that can help you begin to understand the dynamics of the language you use and can provide a vocabulary to help think about this complexity. Texts such as the *Longman English Grammar* (Alexander), organized more like a traditional handbook, can be consulted after a tutoring session to focus on a specific grammar point or trouble area, as when an ESL student wants to know the difference between "I have been living in St. Paul since 1997" and "I have lived in St. Paul since 1997."

It is important to realize that these sources do not necessarily supply an answer that you can simply pass on; instead, they provide information about a language concept that you need in order to start thinking about the next step—how to explain and demonstrate that concept to a writer. If you're looking for help in making this transition, consider an ESL textbook like *How English Works* (Raimes) or *Focus on Grammar* (Maurer) for readable explanations, useful examples, and possible practice activities that can help native and non-native speakers alike. In addition, we highly recommend *The Deluxe Transitive Vampire* (Gorden), not only for a thorough overview of parts of speech, but more importantly because it suggests that grammar examples and even the learning of grammar itself can be creative, humorous, and fun. This is a vital point to keep in mind as you work with any writer.

One area where it is easy to slip back into the "it sounds right" mode is when grammar meets rhetoric. Why do certain pieces of writing just seem to flow while others seem to be derailing? Why does moving information around in a sentence make a paragraph clearer? Books like *Rhetorical Grammar* (Kolln) can help you to understand the grammatical dynamics behind nebulous concepts like "coherence" and "rhythm." Developing a conscious understanding of the principles behind what you frequently do—without thinking—is vital in order to pass this knowledge on to your writers.

And finally, no writer can be without a good dictionary, hardcover or online. *Merriam Webster's Collegiate Dictionary,* 10th ed., is available on CD and works nicely with Windows-based word processing programs.

Knowledge About Practice

Don't ever dream of helping. You have nothing to give. Dream of learning.

Mary Rose O'Reilley,
The Peaceable Classroom

When I (Sandy) first began tutoring, small victories brought me a high. I took pride in helping students learn to overcome stumbling blocks. In short, I enjoyed helping, and I spent much time learning how to do so with tutoring guides such as *The Practical Tutor, Teaching One-to-One,* and *The St. Martin's Sourcebook for Writing Tutors.* From these resources, I learned—and practiced—how to be a successful tutor. Yet, as my mother taught me: it isn't all about you. Studying the act of tutoring is important, but it is equally important to focus on the needs of the writer. Blending knowledge of both tutoring and students will help you achieve a tutoring practice that is informed, personable, and humanistic.

If a successful tutoring session doesn't only focus on helping students with their writing, what does make meaningful tutoring? We have all been in tutoring situations where students tell us of their lives, their losses, their battles, and as human beings, we empathize and want to help them because we have writers, individuals, who come to us needing more than just comma rules. They need to see the value of their writing and to learn about themselves.

Mary Rose O'Reilley's *The Peaceable Classroom* is a great place to start thinking about the writing center as more than just a paper place. The author describes her own students and what she learns through showing them the power of writing. Writers need someone to give them what she calls "a quality of attention" as they share their writing; in other words, they need someone to see them as individuals. A nice companion piece to this book is *The Spiritual Side of Writing* (Paxton and Schiller), a resource that delves further into the act of sharing writing. Essays like "Solitude" (Schiller) can help tutors understand the isolated feelings that many writers associate with the act of academic composing, allowing the tutee's feelings, desires, and needs to impact what we focus on in tutoring practice.

When we meet writers for a tutoring conference, therefore, it is but one part of the composing process. In addition to thinking about their needs as both individuals and writers, we also need to consider how relationships affect writers. Laurel Johnson Black's *Between Talk and Teaching* and Lad Tobin's *Writing Relationships* are two texts that help us think about writing—and conferencing—from the student's perspective. Black focuses on how students can end up either taking notes or becoming active participants in conferences, while Tobin has a more global focus—interpersonal relationships between students and teachers. Both of these books can help us think about how Writing Center theory is not an isolated activity that deals only with the paper at hand or with the students when they are within the walls of the center; tutoring, too, is connected to other facets of composing, learning, and sharing.

In closing, learning about tutoring does not need to be tied to any artificial boundaries. Learn from your own experiences with writing. Learn from the writers who share their words and lives with you. Learn from tutoring. Learn through picking unexpected helpers, one of which might be *The Art of Writing: Teachings of the Chinese Masters* (Barnstone and Ping). This tiny text contains short, crisp sections about writing prose and poetry. Who knows? This could be just the ticket for you and a writer to talk about—whatever!

Knowledge About Students and Tutors

As a writing center tutor, you are constantly encountering difference. Your tutees may differ from you in terms of age, country of origin, ethnicity, culture, socioeconomic class, dialect, gender—the list of possible categories goes on and on. Even with a writer who seems to share your background, there can be an encounter that doesn't work; your discussion operates at crosspurposes, but you are not sure why. Whether they emerge in conversation or on the page, these differences shape—productively or unproductively—the interaction. It is far too easy to see the differences as simply divergence or deviation from a norm—a deficit. Why is that writer so pushy? Why does she sit so close to me? Why doesn't he say what he means? However, there are a variety of resources that can help you begin to theorize about the wider issues of difference and to think about how these issues might affect what you do on a daily basis in the writing center.

Michael Agar's *Language Shock* is an excellent place to start because, though it focuses mainly on how differences work across the intersections of language and culture, it also provides a larger framework through which to think about any differences you encounter. It is also accessible and entertaining. Also, consider looking through some introductory sociolinguistic texts such as Chaika's *Language: The Social Mirror* or McCaulay's *The Social Art: Language and Its Uses.* Because language—spoken and written—is such an important component of a tutoring session, these general discussions of language variation can provide you with new ways of listening to the many different ways people use language.

These resources demonstrate that it is impossible to separate people's linguistic differences from the social and cultural forces that give rise to them. If you want to learn more about how these factors might shape what goes on in the writing center, consider looking at resources that focus more on a specific type of difference. For example, Wolfram's *Dialects in Schools and Communities* or the video *American Tongues* provides useful information about dialects in the United States. Deborah Tannen's *That's Not What I Meant!* explores how social and cultural factors shape conversational styles and the potential miscommunications these styles can create, while *You Just Don't Understand* focuses on how these dynamics often occur between men and women. You will not only see your tutees in these pages, but yourself as well.

Finally, there are a number of resources that can help you explore the notion of difference specifically in terms of writing and teaching. For example, Helen Fox's *Listening to the World* provides a thought-provoking discussion of how the complexity of cultural differences affects students' writing and how easy it is for a teacher/tutor to misread these differences. Similarly, Fan Shen's article "The Classroom and the Wider Culture" offers an insider's look into the difficulties and tensions of composing in a second language. These texts are two of many that explore how writing is often uncomfortably intertwined with issues of identity. When you work with tutees from other countries and/or ethnic backgrounds, the source of difference is perhaps easier to identify. However, Julie Neff's article "Learning Disabilities and the Writing Center" suggests other dimensions that difference can take.

These resources are just a start—one of many possible ways to begin thinking about difference, but they can provide a clearer sense of the bigger issues that lurk beneath the surface of a writing center conference as well as the ones that stare you boldly in the face.

Final Thoughts: Creating Your Own Resources

As we've stressed in this chapter, becoming a resource is much more complex than having a few handbooks on standby for the perfect writing rescue. The experienced tutor knows that there will always be more to learn, and sometimes the most valuable lessons are the ones that we stumble over time and again. Staff meetings and impromptu chats are a crucial component in helping us sift through our experiences and make meaning out of them. Ideally, we would have ample time (and funds) for staff meetings and reflection time between tutoring sessions. Yet reality presents the challenge to us of how to make the ideal possible.

One option is a Tutor Notebook of some kind where you, and every tutor, pen in thoughts for the day. What happened in your tutoring sessions today? What did you think about a certain reading? What did you learn about yourself—or your writing—by talking with a writer? Did you try something new? A Tutor Notebook can be a way of keeping in touch between meetings or getting ideas down while they're fresh. Sometimes, explaining your frustrations over a difficult tutoring session can help you not only understand what happened, but you get advice and empathy from your workmates.

> Hi,
>
> Can I tear my hair out now? I had the most frustrating tutoring session this afternoon. A student handed me his paper and assumed it was my job to make corrections. I tried explaining our philosophy of how the WC works several different ways; no success. Leading questions didn't lead us anywhere. Sadly, I feel like the student left with the same paper he came in with. I really wanted to help him, but I didn't know what to do with his attitude. What else could I have done? What do you all do in this situation? I'll take all the advice I can get!

Collecting shining moments and pressing questions in a Tutor Notebook can be done in any way that fits your unique writing center. An actual journal notebook, a bulletin board of Today's Posts, or even a cyber discussion list could work. Think about the ways that you and your fellow tutors best communicate and work from there. Do you see each other by the coffee maker every day? Maybe a dry erase board or a pegboard could be the starting point. Do you rarely see your centermates? Then perhaps a written journal, print or online, would be the best way to get all of you involved.

Once you have good ideas and suggestions flowing in your writing center, keep them! Since the resources that you will find most helpful depend on your unique writing center and the students who come there, you should try to find some sort of system that will help you keep track of common concerns of both tutors and writers—along with helpful suggestions and useful resources. One option would be a Tutor Resource Collection for your writing center. Setting aside space—a binder or filing cabinet—for these finds allows you to add Web sites, handouts, and tutoring suggestions that you, and all the tutors in your writing center, can develop and share. Some ideas to get you started:

- What is one tip that you received as a new tutor that you find invaluable?
- How do you break the ice with shy writers?
- What is your favorite book or article on tutoring?
- What are your priorities for a tutoring session?
- What is your most successful tutoring strategy? Your most challenging situation?

The possibilities are endless. You can pen tips for tutoring, point out resources that you find enlightening, or create handouts for writers. The best part of a Tutor Resource Collection is that it is flexible and has growth potential. Tutoring may be challenging, but it can also be a collaborative learning experience as well.

In closing, we hope that this chapter is a beginning that will help you think about the types of resources you can use to your best advantage. We also hope you will learn to find the unique resources within yourself. Happy tutoring! May you find your own path and enjoy the journey.

Works Cited

Agar, Michael. 1994. *Language Shock: Understanding the Culture of Conversation.* New York: William Morrow & Co.

Alexander, L. G. 1988. *Longman English Grammar.* New York: Longman Group.

Alvarez, L., and Kolker, A. (Producers). 1987. *American Tongues.* New York: Center for New American Media.

Barnstone, Tony, and Chou Ping, trans. 1996. *The Art of Writing: Teachings of the Chinese Masters.* Boston: Shambhala.

Belanoff, Pat, Betsy Rorschach, and Mia Oberlink. 1993. *The Right Handbook: Grammar and Usage in Context.* 2nd ed. Portsmouth: Boynton Cook Heinemann.

Black, Laurel Johnson. 1998. *Between Talk and Teaching: Reconsidering the Writing Conference.* Logan, Utah: Utah UP.

Chaika, Elaine. 1994. *Language: The Social Mirror,* 3rd ed. Boston: Heinle & Heinle.

Clark, Irene. 1998. *Writing in the Center: Teaching in a WC Setting.* Dubuque: Kendall/ Hunt Publishing.

Drudge, Bob. *My Virtual Reference Desk.* 6 July 1999. <http://www.refdesk.com>.

Fox, Helen. 1994. *Listening to the World: Cultural Issues in Academic Writing.* Urbana, IL: National Council of Teachers of English.

Gorden, Karen E. 1993. *The Deluxe Transitive Vampire: The Ultimate Handbook for the Innocent, the Eager, and the Doomed.* New York: Parthenon.

Greenbaum, Sidney, and Randolph Quirk. 1990. *A Student's Grammar of the English Language.* New York: Longman.

Harris, Muriel. 1986. *Teaching One-to-One: The Writing Conference.* Urbana, IL: National Council of Teachers of English.

Internet Public Library. 6 July 1999. <http://www.ipl.org>.

Kolln, Martha. 1996. *Rhetorical Grammar: Grammatical Choices, Rhetorical Effects.* 2nd ed. Needham Heights, MA: Allyn & Bacon.

Lunsford, Andrea, and Robert Connors. 1997. *The Everyday Writer: A Brief Reference.* New York: St. Martin's Press.

Maurer, Jay. 1995. *Focus on Grammar: An Advanced Course for Reference and Practice.* New York: Addison Wesley Company.

Meyer, Emily, and Louise Z. Smith. 1987. *The Practical Tutor.* New York: Oxford Univ. Press.

Mills, Doug, and Ann Salzmann. *LinguaCenter's Grammar Safari.* 6 July 1999. <http:// deil.lang.uiuc.edu/web.pages/grammarsafari.html>.

Morenberg, Max. 1997. *Doing Grammar,* 2nd ed. New York: Oxford University Press.

Murphy, Christina, and Steve Sherwood. 1995. *The St. Martin's Sourcebook for Writing Tutors.* New York: St. Martin's Press.

Murphy, Christina, Joe Law, and Steve Sherwood, ed. 1996. *Writing Centers: An Annotated Bibliography.* Westport, CT: Greenwood Press.

National Conference on Peer Tutoring in Writing. *NCPTW Homepage.* 1 August 1999. <http://www.chss.iup.edu/wc/ncptw>.

National Writing Centers Association. *NWCA Homepage.* 5 July 1999. 6 July 1999. <http://departments.colgate.edu/diw/NWCAowls.html>.

Neff, Julie. 1994. Learning Disabilities and the Writing Center. In Mullin, Joan A., and Ray Wallace, eds. *Intersections: Theory–Practice in the Writing Center.* Urbana, IL: National Council of Teachers of English.

O'Reilley, Mary Rose. 1993. *The Peaceable Classroom.* Portsmouth, NH: Boynton Cook Heinemann.

Paxton Foehr, Regina, and Susan A. Schiller, eds. 1997. *The Spiritual Side of Writing: Releasing the Learner's Whole Potential.* Portsmouth, NH: Boynton Cook Heinemann.

Purdue University Writing Lab. *Online Writing Lab.* 6 July 1999. <http://owl.english. purdue.edu/>.

Raimes, Ann. 1998. *How English Works: A Grammar Handbook with Readings.* New York: Cambridge University Press.

Ryan, Leigh. 1998. *The Bedford Guide for Writing Tutors.* 2nd ed. Boston: Bedford Books.

Shen, Fan. 1989. "The Classroom and the Wider Culture: Identity as a Key to Learning English Composition." *College Composition and Communication* 40, 459–66.

Sperling, Dave. *Dave's ESL Cafe.* 4 June 1999. 6 July 1999. <http://www.eslcafe.com>.

Tannen, Deborah. 1990. *You Just Don't Understand: Women and Men in Conversation.* New York: William Morrow & Co.

Tannen, Deborah. 1986. *That's Not What I Meant! How Conversational Style Makes or Breaks Your Relations with Others.* New York: Morrow.

Tobin, Lad. 1993. *Writing Relationships: What Really Happens in the Composition Class.* Portsmouth, NH: Boynton Cook Heinemann.

University of Richmond. *Writer's Web.* 6 July 1999. <http://www.urich.edu/~writing/wweb.html>.

Wolfram, Walt, Carolyn Temple Adger, and Donna Christian. 1999. *Dialects in Schools and Communities.* Mahweh, NJ: Lawrence Erlbaum Associates.

Topics for Discussion

The following are topics (related to chapters in this book) that you can talk about in staff meetings, reflect on in a journal, or just ponder. Some of the topics invite you to consider your role as a tutor in the greater college community, some ask thought-provoking questions, and some suggest outside readings.

Topic 1: Doing Something About Bad Assignments

In Chapters 4 and 5, you read about working with unengaged students. To what extent do you feel that students lack a sense of engagement with writing because of dull assignments that are not relevant to them? In the so-called real world, writing grows out of people's actions and beliefs, and it has social and moral consequences. But in school, most writing is done only for assignments, creating a sense of artificiality that is hard to ignore.

One day a teacher wanted to experience his own assignments firsthand, and so he decided that he would do his own writing assignments and turn them in to his students when they turned theirs in to him. He reflected on the experience in an article published in a scholarly journal, from which the following excerpt was taken:

> I remember sitting at my desk one evening when I *had* to get an essay written to give to my students the next morning. I remember the moment clearly. I was sitting there looking at the assignment I had given to my students, when another dark thought came: "I *know* how to write this thing," I remembered saying to myself, "but why in hell would anyone *want* to?"
>
> What I am trying to get at here is that the occasion is wrong. The occasion contains no immediacy; it offers no genuine need that must be genuinely answered. I mean to suggest that even some of our best assignments—imaginative and thoughtful as they may be—do not illicit a driving need to write. I mean to suggest that some of our best assignments do not elicit the students' investment of themselves in the work (emphasis in original).

- From what you've seen in your writing center do you think most writing assignments are relevant to students' lives? What sort of assignments "elicit the students' investment of themselves in the work"? Next time you visit your library, read how Jim Corder answered this question in his article, which remains as relevant today as it was when it was published

25 years ago. ("What I Learned at School" *College Composition and Communication,* Volume 26, Number 4, December 1975)

- Try to envision a writing center that would give regular feedback to instructors about their assignments. As a tutor, would you welcome this opportunity, or not? Before deciding, look at the article "Really Useful Knowledge: A Cultural Studies Agenda for Writing Centers," which appeared in *The Writing Center Journal,* Volume 14, Number 2, 1994, 97–111. In this article Marilyn Cooper explains why she believes that tutors must be a force for change in how writing is taught:

> If tutors want to help students develop agency in writing, they need to cast themselves as radical intellectuals . . . And, yes, I *am* thinking about undergraduate tutors, whose cogent critiques of assignments often leak out in writing center sessions even when they don't make them explicit. Furthermore, in helping students become agents of their own writing, tutors also become agents of change in writing pedagogy, helping teachers create better assignments, letting teachers know what students are having trouble with. As intellectuals, tutors contribute both to the endeavor of helping students learn about writing and to the endeavor of creating useful knowledge about writing. (emphasis in original)

- Students sometimes want to write on topics that many instructors discourage or disallow—their religious faith, political beliefs, sexual preferences or experiences, high school achievements, drug use, roommate problems, and so on. As you read in Chapter 3, these can be emotionally charged topics, making it difficult for instructors and tutors to read and respond. And yet these topics can be highly relevant to students' lives. If students were to bring papers on such topics into your writing center, could you handle it? Would reading such papers better enable you to provide instructors with what Cooper (see quote above) calls "really useful knowledge" about what's important to students?

Topic 2: Due Process for Plagiarism

Chapter 14 in this book reminds us that writing center tutors are never very far away from dealing with issues of plagiarism. If a student on your campus has been accused of plagiarism by a professor, where can he turn for help? On most campuses students have few options when they are in this situation. If your campus has a policy on cheating, plagiarism is probably included. Get a copy of the policy and see whether it clearly defines plagiarism, describes the procedure of due process for the accused, and lists the possible penalties. Does the judicial board that handles violations of this policy also provide advisement for the student to ensure that his rights are upheld?

In many ways, writing centers are uniquely situated to play a role in educating students about the campus policy on plagiarism and working to see that it is fair, current, and followed. Some students might even wish that the writing center would go further and advise them, or perhaps even be their advocates, if they were to be accused of plagiarism. Can you envision your writing center becoming a resource (see Chapter 15) for serving students in this way? If it were to do so, do you think there would be more or fewer cases of plagiarism on your campus?

Topic 3: The Idea of a Radical Writing Center

This topic can be related to the ideas you read about in Chapters 6 and 7 concerning individual style, developing one's voice, and breaking rules. It's a radical idea, but bear with me for a while. Imagine the writing center as a place where students who are considered different, either because of their skin color or ethnicity or other background, could speak to a tutor about maintaining— rather than eliminating—nonstandard ways of writing.

Try thinking about it this way. Regardless of your background, as an undergraduate you probably realized at some point that college changes you. New ideas and exposure to different people, styles, and habits can influence you in subtle ways. It's especially apparent when you return home and realize that hometown friends and family haven't changed—you have. Then at some point, you realize that it's nice to be able to have both a college life and a hometown life. For the visits to uncle Ned's, you remove the nose ring and modify your language. But this doesn't mean you're going mainstream. You are just projecting different roles and identities when you choose to.

For some students of color, some students who come from urban or rural areas, or some students who are regarded as different for whatever reason, there is the same desire to hold onto and project their various roles and identities when they choose to. However, college tends to put greater pressure on them to deny certain identities than it puts on mainstream middle-class, white students for whom society tends to be more tolerant. Example: students who speak nonstandard forms of English—and they may be rural white students as well as urban nonwhites—are often taught at home and at school that standard written English is the one correct way to speak and write and any deviation from it will mark them as inferior when they are away from home. Meanwhile, middle-class, white students learn that using college slang or trying out a new voice or style is OK—different, but OK. A part of growing up, and certainly not a mark of inferiority or a lack of education. From this double-standard, nonmajority students learn that to be accepted among teachers and employers, they have to write and speak even more correctly—more standard—than their majority counterparts (usually middle-class whites). For them, breaking the rules and experimenting with different styles of writing is riskier because the mainstream culture tends to judge them more critically for behaving differently. As Min-zhan Lu writes, "Mastery of academic discourses is often accompanied by a change in one's point of view" and "in the way one perceives the world . . . and relates to it." p. 332 (quoted in Bawarshi and Pelkowski, p. 49).

An article in a recent issue of *The Writing Center Journal* (Bawarshi, Anis and Stephanie Pelkowski, "Postcolonialism and the Idea of a Writing Center." *The Writing Center Journal* 19 (2) (1999), 41–58) proposes the idea of a writing center that would help marginalized students to see how academic writing has the potential to change their point of view and how they relate to their home culture and the world. The point is not to turn any student away from standard writing, the authors argue, but "to teach them how to preserve their multiple, even conflicting social roles while doing so" (p. 54).

- Try to imagine a writing center that functioned in this way. It should, according to the authors, encourage students to think critically about the underlying assumptions of standard English: Why do the rules exist? Who is served by them? Who is not?

- Do you like the idea of this kind of writing center? Would students want to come here for help?

Topic 4: Would an Experienced Writing Tutor Do This?

Chapter 2 talks about ways for tutors to avoid crossing the line and doing the wrong thing when helping writers. Here are some things that can happen in a writing center. For each one, explain whether you think an experienced tutor would do it, or would consider it to be crossing the line.

1. Help a student compose a grade appeal
2. Eat a snack while the student rewrites his conclusion
3. Read a student's paper aloud if the student says she does not want to read it herself
4. Agree to type up a writer's paper
5. Suggest a better title for a writer's paper
6. Politely tell a writer that he or she is offended by something the writer has written
7. Tell a writer that parts of the paper sound as though they were copied
8. Let a writer know that she agrees with him that an instructor's assignment seems unreasonable
9. Organize a protest against required attendance in freshman composition
10. Encourage a writer who wanted to try out an unconventional style to do so

Topic 5: Know Thy Self

Many chapters in this book (1, 2, 9, 10, 15 and others) make the point that to be a good tutor, you always have to try to step back, look at your job from different perspectives, and ask yourself questions like, How do I appear to the students who come to me for help? How do I know when I'm in over my head with a student's paper? How can I tell when we're on the right track? Some years ago, Rafoth and Murphy conducted a study of 14 expert tutors (as identified by their directors) from writing centers around the country (Rafoth, B. A. and E. K. Murphy, "Expertise in Tutoring." *Maryland English Journal* 29 (1) (Fall 1994), 1–9). They interviewed the tutors about various aspects of their jobs, and posed this question to them:

How do you know when a tutoring session is going well?

Most tutors answered that they felt a session was going well when the student did most of the talking. But think about this for a minute. Is this really a good indicator of whether or not a tutoring session is going well? Why do you think these tutors answered the question this way? And finally, how do *you* know when a tutoring session is going well?

Which of the following would you consider indicative of a session that is going well? Which ones not so well, or headed for derailing?

1. The writer is the one doing most of the talking.

2. The writer is very nervous and unsure of herself throughout the session.

3. The writer writes down everything you say.

4. You find the writer's ideas to be personally offensive, and he wants to know how to make his arguments even stronger.

5. The writer pulls out a paper marked with a D grade and a note from the instructor that says, "Go to the Writing Center and re-submit for a possible higher grade."

6. After you have gone over a few things together with him, the writer asks you if another tutor is available.

Topic Six: Ignore Your Audience?

In the chapters of this book and in most books about writing, there is one piece of advice tutors and teachers seem to give writers more than any other: "Think of your audience." It seems so all important, so profound, so obvious. How could it *not* be the best advice in the world?

In fact, there is some debate among writing theorists about the role that audience awareness plays in the writing process. One of the most well-known writing teachers in the business, Peter Elbow, has written that it might actually be a good thing for writers to ignore their audience once in a while, especially when being aware of an audience actually seems to inhibit the writer. He likens this to the problem of being in the presence of people who always make us feel dumb when we try to speak to them (some teachers, for example); we can't seem to find the right words or thoughts, even when we want to. If we are writing to an audience that we imagine to be second guessing us all the time, it can cause us to write things we don't really mean or want to say, or it can dry up the creative juices and give us a case of writer's block, or it can just push us into sounding too cute and clever or into using words that sound OK but say nothing. When this happens, says Elbow, it's time to ignore the audience, think about what it is that *you* want to say, and write it.

As a tutor, you may disagree with Elbow's ideas about audience. Perhaps you have worked with writers who are more clueless than they are intimidated by an audience. In any case, I hope you'll find Elbow's idea to be thought provoking. You might think about whether your own sense of audience awareness tends to get in the way sometimes when you write, or why some of the papers you read in the writing center sound so stilted. Talk with other tutors and ask them to reflect on the role that audience awareness plays in their writing. Finally, I highly recommend reading the article in which Elbow explains his ideas about audience. You'll find it is very readable and more thought provoking than I'm able to convey here:

Elbow, Peter. January 1987. "Closing My Eyes as I Speak: An Argument for Ignoring Audience." *College English* 49 (1), 50–69.

Contributors

Corinne Agostinelli is a marketing coordinator with Pennsylvania Financial Group in State College, Pennsylvania. During the academic year, she continues to work part time as a peer writing consultant for a Hospitality Communications class at Pennsylvania State University, where she graduated in 1998 with a Bachelor of Arts degree in English (emphasis in Creative Writing.) Corinne spent two years as a writing tutor at Penn State and presented at both National and Mid-Atlantic Writing Center conferences.

Wendy Bishop teaches rhetoric and composition and creative writing at Florida State University. She directed the writing center at the University of Alaska Fairbanks before moving to Tallahassee in 1989. From 1989 to 1992, she directed the first-year writing program at FSU.

Kara Bui worked as an English peer tutor at the University of Michigan's Sweetland Writing Center for two years and received her B.S. degree in cellular molecular biology. During that time, she also managed communications between tutors and clients for Sweetland's Online Writing Laboratory.

George Cooper is a lecturer in the Sweetland Writing Center at the University of Michigan. In addition to the seminar in peer tutoring, he teaches composition and studies writing assessment and the history of composition.

Mary Mortimore Dossin teaches writing at Plattsburgh State University of New York and trained and supervised the writing tutors there for fifteen years. She has recently retired from writing center work to give time to her personal writing. Mary Dossin hosted the National Conference on Peer Tutoring in Writing in 1998.

Sandy Eckard began her tutoring experience as an intern in the Writing Center at Frostburg State University. While completing her doctoral studies at Indiana University of Pennsylvania, she held a graduate assistantship in IUP's Writing Center. In addition to teaching at Frostburg State, she is currently writing her dissertation, entitled *The Ties That Bind: Analyzing Storytelling in Composition Classrooms and Writing Centers.*

Alexis Greiner is a recent graduate from Rollins College, where she was an interdisciplinary studies major in biology, philosophy, and writing, and was a two-year veteran of the Writing Center. She was selected a Clough Consultant, a leader and example within the center, and was voted Writing Consultant of the Year in 1999. Alexis gave the keynote address at the National Conference on Peer Tutoring in Writing in Lexington, Kentucky, in 1997. She plans to pursue a career that will utilize the skills she developed as a writing consultant.

Muriel Harris is professor of English and the Writing Lab Director at Purdue University, where she has tutored and trained tutors for over twenty years. Her handbook,

Prentice Hall Reference Guide to Grammar and Usage (now in its 4th edition), and also *The Writer's FAQs* (Prentice Hall, forthcoming), a brief pocket manual, are both products of her writing center experience. Her articles, book chapters, and conference presentations all reflect her commitment to the tutorial approach as the most effective way to help writers.

William J. Macauley, Jr. directs the Writing Tutorial Lab and is an Assistant Professor of English at Purdue University Calumet, where he also teaches courses in composition, literature, and technical writing. He earned his Ph.D. degree in Rhetoric and Linguistics in 1999 from Indiana University of Pennsylvania; his dissertation studied studio-based learning, student empowerment, and composition. He learned a great deal about how to teach writing by working as a writing tutor.

Lea Masiello is Director of Liberal Studies English and a professor in the Department of English at Indiana University of Pennsylvania. She was codirector of the IUP Writing Center for ten years during which time she was also a faculty member in IUP's Learning Center. She enjoys helping make connections between the Writing Center and English courses that all IUP students must take.

Helena Poch attends Temple University School of Law. She graduated from Pennsylvania State University in 1999 with a Bachelor of Science degree in Nursing and a minor in World Literature. Helena worked for the Penn State Writing Center for three-and-a-half years and presented at two national conferences. She continues to write and enjoys helping others realize their writing potential.

Ben Rafoth directs the Writing Center at Indiana University of Pennsylvania. He teaches courses in research methods and composition theory and pedagogy. His other publications include books and journal articles on teaching writing.

Linda Riker is a 1998 graduate of the University of Michigan, where she received a Bachelor of Science degree in Biology. She plans to pursue a career in marine biology and also enjoys swimming, reading, and mountain biking.

Jennifer J. Ritter is a doctoral student in Rhetoric and Linguistics at Indiana University of Pennsylvania, where she also gained experience as a tutor in the IUP Writing Center. She designed and developed IUP's Online Writing Center. Her interests include second-langauge acquisition and English as a Second Language instruction.

Elizabeth Santoro is a law student at William and Mary. She graduated from Pennsylvania State University in 1999 with a Bachelor of Arts degree in International Politics and a B.A. in French. At Penn State she was a tutor and cocoordinator of the Writing Center.

Jennifer E. Staben's first experiences as a tutor at the University of Iowa's Writing Lab in 1991 led her to shift her educational focus from literature to language and literacy. She has since taught courses in composition, ESL, and study skills and has been involved with writing centers at the College of Lake County in Illinois and the College of St. Catherine in St. Paul, Minnesota. She is currently a doctoral student at Indiana University of Pennsylvania where she worked as a writing center tutor and as an instructor at the American Language Institute. Her research interests include literacy, ESL writers, and writing centers.

Alice Trupe directs the Writing Center and teaches in the English Department at Bridgewater College of Virginia. Her other writing and research interests revolve around the impact of electronic environments on genre and pedagogy.

Molly Wingate has been the director of the Colorado College Writing Center since 1987. She writes about tutor training and writing center administration. She is a long-time member of the board of the National Conference on Peer Tutoring in Writing (NCPTW) and a member of NCTE and CCCC. In 1999, she won the Ron Maxwell Award from the NCPTW for her leadership in promoting the collaborative learning practices of peer tutoring in writing.

Beth Rapp Young directs the University Writing Center at the University of Central Florida in Orlando, where she also teaches courses in writing, grammar, and research methods. In the past, she has directed or tutored in writing centers at the University of Alabama in Huntsville, Rollins College, and the University of Southern California. She currently serves on the board of the Southeastern Writing Centers Association and the National Conference on Peer Tutoring in Writing.

INDEX